MW01122235

STUDIES IN AMERICAN POPULAR HISTORY AND CULTURE

Edited by
Jerome Nadelhaft
University of Maine

A ROUTLEDGE SERIES

Studies in American Popular History and Culture

Jerome Nadelhaft, *General Editor*

US Textile Production in Historical Perspective

A Case Study from Massachusetts

Susan M. Ouellette

Routledge
New York & London

An earlier version of Chapter 1 was published as "Divine Providence and Collective Endeavor: Sheep Production in Early Massachusetts," *New England Quarterly*, Vol. LXIX, No. 3, Sept. 1996: 355–380. Reprinted with permission.

Routledge
Taylor & Francis Group
270 Madison Avenue
New York, NY 10016

Routledge
Taylor & Francis Group
2 Park Square
Milton Park, Abingdon
Oxon OX14 4RN

© 2007 by Taylor & Francis Group, LLC
Routledge is an imprint of Taylor & Francis Group, an Informa business

Printed in the United States of America on acid-free paper
10 9 8 7 6 5 4 3 2 1

International Standard Book Number-10: 0-415-97988-9 (Hardcover)
International Standard Book Number-13: 978-0-415-97988-7 (Hardcover)

Library of Congress Cataloging-in-Publication Data

Ouellette, Susan.
   US textile production in historical perspective : a case study from Massachusetts / Susan M. Ouellette.
      p. cm. -- (Studies in American popular history and culture)
   Includes bibliographical references and index.
   ISBN 0-415-97988-9
   1. Textile industry--Massachusetts--History. I. Title. II. Title: U.S. textile production in historical perspective. III. Series: American popular history and culture (Routledge (Firm))

HD9857.M4O94 2006
338.4'767700973--dc22   2006015205

Visit the Taylor & Francis Web site at
http://www.taylorandfrancis.com

and the Routledge Web site at
http://www.routledge-ny.com

Contents

List of Charts

Introduction

Current historical wisdom regarding the settlement and economic growth of seventeenth-century New England describes a colony perennially dependent on external sources of manufactured goods. In this model of scarcity, the first waves of Great Migration colonists were the primary sources of provisions, manufactured goods, cash and credit. When the regular arrival of newcomers waned, the colony shifted its dependence to a sea-based merchant fleet. These blue water traders created networks along which manufactured goods and marketable surplus circulated. Naturally, New England's colonies would have floundered and died without those merchants. Despite ample regular food supplies provided by the farms and fields of New England, the colonies continued to require vast exports of manufactured goods from Old England to fulfill its needs. As one historian observed,

> [In the beginning,] as long as hundreds of emigrant families disembarked at New England ports each year, the region's economic survival seemed assured. The newcomers' stores . . . added wealth to a colonial economy that could not depend on the lucrative staple crops that supported [other] British settlements. . . . Once emigration ceased . . . the precariousness of such economic arrangements was fully revealed and New England suffered its first economic depression.[1]

Thus, the end of the Great Migration period in 1642 brought the first phase of successful settlement to a close. At the same time, colonial officials recognized that New England would have to develop a sustainable economy on its own or it would not survive.

Hampered by the paucity of export staples, New England's leaders struggled to find a way to balance the demand for manufactured goods against the relative penury of the northeastern colonies. At first, colonial

1

governments attempted to foster home-based manufactures by establishing production bounties, trade monopolies and other forms of encouragement. These efforts met with only "mixed success."[2] Finally, it was the sea-based merchants who forged the important links between West Indian sugar plantations, New England's food surplus and English credit.

> Throughout the colonial period the merchants—those who dealt for personal profit in the wholesale import, export, and distribution of goods—were the dynamic economic force in the northern colonies. . . . *[O]verseas trade alone could furnish the settlers with the materials needed for maintaining reasonably comfortable lives.* . . . [my emphasis] [Since] the natural goods of New England largely duplicated the produce of England, exchanges were to be made in places outside of England and profits to be translated into credits in England.[3]

Thus, elite merchants led the way to the success of the New England colonies where all else failed. With a lucrative trade network in place, New England colonists concentrated on farming and raising livestock, which provided modest, but tangible gains.

Certainly, the achievement of those bold merchant mariners can hardly be denied. Yet, New England's economic success cannot be fully explained by this model. Ironware and textiles were among the most sought after manufactured products in the colony and colonists knew this to be true before they emigrated. In the first years of the "Great Migration" period, colonists and English investors joined together to develop New England industry for profits and to meet those vital needs. Early iron manufactories did poorly in the seventeenth century, especially in Massachusetts. The Hammersmith forge at Saugus floundered and then failed, but not because the established ironworks failed to produce ironware. Rather, active production of tons of raw iron and the manufacture of ironware products at Hammersmith and Braintree failed to yield the desired cash profits to investors in England. One problem was the type of ore available to New Englanders in the period. Bog ore needed to be mined in great quantities to produce small amounts of raw iron. The second and even more serious problem was the difficulty of transferring profits to England. The local market could support iron production only when producers accepted payment in kind. The disappointed investors found that the grain, livestock and food supplies offered in payment did not translate into wealth as easily as Southern tobacco, indigo or rice. Poor revenues combined with poor management ultimately forced most of the Bay Colony iron manufactories into bankruptcy. There, the lesson taught by the failure of these iron manufactories was that the infant economy of

New England could not sustain any industry that required a heavy outlay in equipment, land and skilled labor while investors were not willing to wait for their profits.[4]

The production of textiles differed markedly from the production of raw iron or finished ironware, but the local market focus and economic outcome of provincial cloth production was quite similar. Despite the desire of some that textiles develop into an exportable commodity, textile products circulated almost exclusively within the local economy in the seventeenth- and into the eighteenth-century. This is not to say that textile production was unimportant or small-scale; rather, the regional effects of this production were profound and affected every man, woman and child who lived in New England.

Just as finished cloth from England came with the first waves of emigrants to the seventeenth-century New England, the skills and tools necessary for textile work crossed the ocean with every ship. Many came directly from textile-producing regions of Old England and intended to apply their expertise in the new land right away. Compared to the small contingent of Scottish prisoners of war forced to labor in a few New England ironworks, skilled clothmakers were a significant portion of every town's population. Also significant, they did not arrive empty-handed. The portable nature of textile tools made it possible for many of them to be transported to the colonies. In addition, the relatively simple construction of some tools meant they could easily be made from indigenous materials. Finally, textile fibers could be produced nearly anywhere the colonists went, not just near certain areas like iron bogs. Wherever sheep could be raised or hemp and flax sown, cloth could be made, coarse or fine.

One of the most powerful forces to influence New England textile work was cultural tradition. A deeply embedded practice of cottage-produced "rough" or homespun cloth existed among the early settlers that dated far back into their past.[5] In seventeenth-century England, housewives regularly circumvented middlemen and merchants by producing much of their household's textile needs, simultaneously saving money and supplementing the family budget. As one contemporary agricultural tract observed:

> Undoubted a woman cannot get her livinge honestly with spinning on
> the dystaffe, but it stoppeth a gap and must needs be had.[6]

Colonial housewives could also take up their distaffs and wheels to provide much-needed rough cloth for the same reasons. Yet American historians regularly cite "evidence" contrary to such a notion:

There were . . . serious problems with the supply of materials to turn
into fabric. Although thousands of sheep were imported into New England they were slow to thrive . . . ,the docile sheep were no match
for preditors—particularly wolves. . . . Few families bothered with
sheep rearing. [Despite official pressure to produce hemp and flax,
they] never became mainstays of textile production either. Efforts to
import West Indian cotton likewise amounted to little.[7]

According to this logic, rather than establish a provincial textile
industry, frugal colonists continued to import cloth or turned to conservative measures like "careful mending and passing down of clothing from
one generation to the next."[8] Most of all, the endemic shortage of labor
absorbed any would-be textile producers into the more necessary activities of colony building. In short, cattle, grains, and wood were simply better economic investments for New Englanders than flax, hemp or sheep.
Exports, after all, were the stuff economic security and market economies
were based upon.

Indeed, the depression of the 1640s propelled New England merchants on to the sea and ultimately facilitated their blue water entrepre-
neurial success. Moreover, salted beef and fish, oak barrel staves and other
New England products provided the foundation for the exchange of West
Indian produce as well as English manufactured goods. To imagine, however, that New England's economic growth rested solely on these products
neglects the importance of the expanding internal economy of the colony.

Likewise, such a conclusion ignores a large body of evidence pointing
to a major provincial textile industry that encompassed both professional
weavers and vernacular "cottage" weavers in the colony. Probate inventories of the period contain multiple references to fabrics of all types that
indicate a substantial volume of textiles flowed from the wheels and looms
of colonial households and workshops.

It is quite true that the making of cloth was a labor-intensive process. Considerable volumes of production, a particular distribution of labor
activities and varying degrees of skill were needed to transform raw fibers
into serviceable cloth. However, this does not necessarily lead to the conclusion that all textiles were imported. Rather, the very nature of colonial society made the production of textiles, simple and fancy, inevitable, especially
if the conditions allowed for its production. One contemporary observer
remarked in 1643: "In prospering hemp and flax so well it is frequently sown,
spun, and woven into linnen cloth; and so, with cotton wooll . . . and
our linen yarn we can make dimities and fustians for our summer clothing;
and . . . we hope to have woolen cloth [as well] . . ."[9]

As noted above, the typical colonial wardrobe required several different qualities and types of fabric: linen, cotton and woolens of varying weights and weaves.[10] Thus, Bailyn's observation that the volume of woolens produced could only "ultimately" measure the "success of the textile industry" is flawed. His assertion that "cotton and linen fabrics would not suffice [as clothing] for settlers during chilly autumns and long, bitter winters" demonstrates a limited understanding of the importance of all types of fabrics to everyday life.[11] Certainly clothing was important. Consider the probate inventory presented to the Salem court in 1677 by Robert Wilkes' neighbors, John Hill and William Woodbery. Included in the inventory is a list of Wilkes' clothing; this list provides us with an illustration of the typical wardrobe of an average householder. A heavy wool cloak, twill coat, waistcoat and trousers probably represented his best clothing. A "jackit and briches . . . stokins and shues . . . [and several changes of] wearing linging" was his every day clothing. None of the descriptions of Wilkes clothing indicate that it was imported cloth. In fact, the absence of descriptive labels such as "Holland," "Irish" or "Pennistone" implies a provincial origin. More importantly, Wilkes' wardrobe consisted of linen, cotton/linen and wool cloth of different weights; this variety indicates the range of available fabrics as well as their use.[12]

The average woman's wardrobe was, to some extent, more varied than a man's. Phebe Eaton, a widow who lived in Haverhill, owned "a penniston petticoat, cotton petticoat, carsee (kersey) petticoat, two wascuts (waistcoats), cloth hood, small linging, a blacke cap and neck cloth, two hatts, a stuffe gound, a paire shooes and stokins."[13] Again, as in Wilkes' clothing, most of the pieces were probably fashioned from locally produced cloth. Her best petticoat, made of English Penniston wool was most certainly made of imported cloth, while her kersey and linen things were everyday wear and probably woven in a local workshop—or even a neighbor's home—judging from their valuation. Again, Phebe Eaton's wardrobe demonstrates the variety of fabrics, weaves and fibers of a typical wardrobe while it contained only one piece of clothing clearly identified and valued as imported.

By modern standards both Wilkes' and Eaton's probate inventories recount a sparse collection of clothing. However, many hours of work were represented in those few garments: twenty or more yards of woven cloth was required for each full suit of clothing and literally miles of yarn spun in order to produce them.[14] Purchasing locally manufactured cloth or utilizing household labor to produce cloth considerably reduced the necessity of substantial outlays of scarce coin or extensions of precious English credit for clothing. In addition, the outlay for fabric made in the colonies was less because there were fewer middlemen to pay and no shipping costs. Finally, locally produced cloth meant that individuals benefited from these neighborhood exchanges through community controls placed on prices and the face to face negotiation with their neighbors for produce or labor to get what they needed.

The need for good clothing was perpetual and clothes were precious. As already observed, many probate inventory records of the period listed items of clothing passed down to family members like heirlooms. Yet, clothing eventually wore out beyond mending and, as every housewife probably knew to her dismay, new stockings were constantly required. In the case of growing children, the problem of keeping them adequately dressed was often critical. Beyond basic clothing needs, there were other, perhaps even more important requirements for cloth as well. Linen sheets, pillow covers, bed ticking for mattress covers, woolen blankets, and wool coverlets were necessary household items, even in lesser households. Bed furnishings, curtains and hangings, provided much needed protection in a time of no central heating, insulation or efficiently glazed window openings. In the kitchen, daily activities called for table linens, toweling, grain and flour sacks, cheesecloth, pudding wraps and other fabrics whose use is long forgotten. Most households also contended with infants' needs including diaper cloths and childbirth linens. Still other probate inventories listed items such as lap robes, horse blankets, saddle pads, seed sacks and feed bags. All over New England probate records reveal that cloth was an essential part of everyday life; a lack of cloth had far more profound consequences than simply a lack of warm clothing. A rough estimate using 75 probate records between 1655 and 1675 for Massachusetts Bay, Plymouth Colony and Rhode Island with itemized clothing and fabric goods' descriptions underscores that necessity.

On average, each household contained housekeeping items of approximately 65 yards of linen or linen/cotton fabric. Additional yardage devoted to clothing indicates that 30 to 40 yards of wool, linen, and linen/cotton fabric was necessary to clothe each adult member of the household. Thus the average fabric needs of each adult were approximately 50 yards of fabric. With an estimated population of 33,000 in 1665, this would mean that New Englanders required approximately 1.6 million yards of cloth.[15]

Given the ordinary quality of most textile needs, it seems unlikely that the colony's cash-poor economy could afford or would even attempt to import such simple, but voluminous needs. This is not to say that imported cloth did not circulate in the colonial economy. As we have seen in the case of Phebe Eaton, these can be found with some regularity in the records as well. Certainly in the probates of wealthy merchants such as Henry

Shrimpton of Boston or Phillip English of Salem, imported fabric figured largely in their household's wealth. Beyond Massachusetts, the same pattern emerges in the records. As one Rhode Islander, William Harris, observed, " . . . the better sort of Linnen is brought from England." Harris also contended that despite the preference for fine English linen, much of the woolen, linsey-woolsey and cotton-woolen cloth was produced locally by highly skilled spinners and weavers.[16] Indeed, Harris' observations reveal a vibrant provincial textile industry and one that had surprising economic ramifications. In the probate sample described above, at least half of the fabrics, especially among the poorer folk were "coarse." Even a conservative estimate indicates that New Englanders potentially produced over 800,000 yards of fabrics or, in probate values, about £40,000.

Although historians have tended to minimize the manufacture of textiles in the pre-industrial era, New England most certainly possessed the means to produce vast quantities of textiles: sheep, water, flax, tools and most important, textile skills and labor. Despite the depredations of wolves on the livestock of New England, the numbers of sheep grew steadily throughout the period studied. Evidence gleaned from probate records, town selectmen meetings and official colonial records as well as the private and published writings of individuals bear this out. Very early in the life of the colonies, wool was available for the manufacture of woolen cloth, if only on a small scale at first. After all, if "the few families who bothered with sheep . . . [produced enough wool] to support the domestic production of homespun," what else would the average household desire?[17]

Equally available, perhaps even more so at first, was flax and hemp for the manufacture of linens. Flax and hemp seed were easily transported, far more so than livestock, and seem to have grown well. New England's soils, though not as fertile as colonists hoped, produced flax readily and continually throughout the period studied. Likewise, the "plentiful growth of wild hemp" in the colony was there for the colonists' gathering. Combined with a considerable supply of English and Spanish cotton purchased in the West Indies, a whole range of cloth was possible: pure linen, pure cotton, dimities, diaper, fustians and other combinations of linen and cotton needful in the average English household.

As observed earlier, textile tools and skills came with the colonists to New England. In at least one instance, Rowley, a woolen-producing town in Yorkshire transplanted a portion of its inhabitants to Rowley, Massachusetts, in New England. These Yorkshire men and women did not come to change their lifestyle, they intended to perpetuate it. The first to do so in New England, Rowley men built a fulling mill to process their wool cloth even as they built gristmills and sawmills to service the town's milling and sawing needs.[18] Rowley women most certainly set about providing and processing the raw materials for their husbands' craft as evidenced by the surviving account books of the Pearson mill.

Here again, conventional wisdom has obscured rather than revealed. Much has been written about the labor "shortage" in early New England. According to this logic, the ideal labor pool, young, able-bodied, single men, immigrated to the Chesapeake. This deprived New England of a much-needed source of economic growth potential. However, this notion disregards New England's intensive use of the labor of women and children, a labor pool of great abundance and potential in relatively stable, healthy agricultural communities. Moreover, the healthy environment of New England made the size of families and length of productive years greater than anywhere in British North America. So, the labor "shortage" of New England is a false one when evaluating the development of certain provincial industries, especially textile production. By discounting the labor of women and children, historians have ignored much of the productive potential of New England.

Most significant, the textile work dovetailed well with the rhythms of colonial farm life. The processes leading up to the weaving of cloth (and including the simpler weaving) could be broken down into simple tasks. Thus, the work could be placed aside when necessary and taken up again quite easily. This was ideal for women and children whose lives revolved around the demands of childcare, housework and farm chores. Rather than "an occasional occupation of . . . farmers and petty artisans who bought almost all their textiles from . . . importers or from middlemen," textile production occurred around and between the seasonal labors of New England colonists, especially married women and their daughters.[19]

Yet, textile production was not solely the activity of women and children. As we shall see, the making of cloth was a shared venture between men and women, children and parents. Although women dominated some aspects of textile work, most notably the preparation of fibers and spinning of yarn, both men and women shared different responsibilities at each stage of production. Master weavers, who were most certainly male in this period, worked alongside their wives and children who often wove the simpler fabrics requiring less skill. Indeed, the making of textiles wove the sexes together in their daily labors as surely as the weaver intertwined the warp and weft threads of his fabric.

It may be difficult for us to understand the profound influence of textile work on the lives of New Englanders, but it was wholly obvious to them. Edward Taylor, a Puritan minister in Westfield, Massachusetts, employed his understanding of textile work as a metaphor for a spiritually

satisfying life. In his poem, "Huswifery," Taylor applied the homely details
of cloth making to his own life as a man of God:

> Make me, O Lord, thy Spinning Wheel complete.
> Thy Holy Worde my Distaff make for me,
> Make my Soule thy holy Spoole to bee.
> My conversation make to be thy Reele
> And reele the yarn thereon spun of thy Wheele.
>
> Make me thy Loome then, knit therin this twine:
> And make thy Holy Spirit, Lord, winde quills:
> Then weave the Webb thyelfe. The yarn is fine.
> Thine Ordinances make my Fulling Mills.
> Then dy the same in Heavenly Colours Choice,
> All pinkt with Varnisht Flowers of Paradise.
>
> Then cloath therewith mine Understanding, Will,
> Affections, Judgment, Conscience, Memory
> My Words, and Actions, that their shine may fill
> My wayes with glory and thee glorify.
> Then mine apparell shall display before yee
> That I am Cloathd in Holy robes for glory.[20]

In Edward Taylor's household, textile production was associated with
the very meaning of life.

In other New England households, the work may not have held the
spiritual significance of Taylor's poem, but was still a potentially powerful
social force. As skills and tools passed from one generation to the next, the
connections spread across time as well as space. Moreover, one household
could not produce independently of another, causing the threads of production to weave neighborhoods, communities and, ultimately, the colony into
elaborate patterns of reciprocity and inter-dependence. Such production may
only occasionally have become a part of any publicly recorded transaction,
but as part of the landscape of barter and exchange, textiles became one area
of production that enabled colonists to move closer to their ideals of com-
petence and self-reliance. Thus, in order to really understand the early social
and economic history of New England, historians must not only reinstate
women and children as actors in the historical landscape, but must also com-
prehend how pre-industrial men and women cooperated in their endeavors.

This study re-examines traditional sources such as probate inventories, wills, account books and diaries for evidence of textile manufacture in

early New England. Close reading of probate inventories in the years 1630–1700 reveals the availability and production of textiles among the households recorded and even suggests the organization of production among those households. Wills, account books and diaries, although concentrated on the male activities of their authors, disclose other minutiae that clearly link their families with much of the labor required to manufacture textiles. Town selectmen records and other official records provide important insights in the management of community resources, especially those pertaining to textile manufacture. Agricultural tracts and other related works provide even more clues to those processes. Taken together, the recorded glimpses of textile production in New England communities provide an opportunity to explore a submerged economy that shaped the larger social and economic structures of early New England even as it supported the daily needs of individual households.

Chapter One
Sheep Flocks and Wool Harvests

"The Lord has been pleased to increase sheep extraordinarily of late"
—Captain Edward Johnson, 1642[1]

In his New World narrative, *Wonder-Working Providence of Sion's Savior in New England*, Captain Edward Johnson described the material wealth accumulated by his fellow colonists between the years 1628 and 1651 with great detail. In terms nearly as reverent although not as poetic as Edward Taylor, Johnson extolled the phenomenal growth of Massachusetts' livestock herds. His interest is not surprising. In the agricultural economy of early New England, domestic animals were an essential ingredient which, when combined with land, became a primary source of wealth and prosperity. Moreover, an abundance of domestic animals guaranteed the future growth and prosperity of the new settlements.[2]

In Johnson's estimation, the population growth of Bay Colony livestock was nothing less than miraculous:

> There are supposed to be in Massachusetts [Bay] government at this day [1651], . . . about fifteen thousand acres in tillage, . . . cattell about twelve thousand neate, and about three thousand sheepe.[3]

The expanding population of Massachusetts' domestic animals fired Johnson's imagination and he was especially jubilant over the sheep flock for although "cattell" provided food and leather products, sheep's wool provided much-needed warm clothing and bedding. Describing the prolific growth of sheep in the colony as "extraordinary" proof of divine approval, Johnson pointed out that access to woolen cloth "hath not been cut short" and uncertain supplies from England were about to become a specter of the past.

Divine approval was not restricted to the Bay Colony. The sheep populations in Rhode Island and Connecticut dramatically expanded in the seventeenth century as well. A 1654 observation held that there were "thousands in Rhode Island." Willingness on the part of Rhode Islanders to export their surplus into Connecticut assured those farmers of a steady supply from their neighbor's flocks.[4]

For an infant economy struggling to cope with debt and the vagaries of sea-based supply lines, this was welcome news. Johnson's 1651 estimate forecast a ready supply of over six tons of raw wool in Massachusetts for that year with a potential doubling of each year's harvest thereafter.[5] John Higgenson, the New Haven farmer responsible for the 1654 assessment, forecasted a similar yield for Rhode Island.[6] Reserves of such magnitude permitted more than an adequate basis for domestic textile manufacture of a considerable scope.[7] Sheep and wool were extremely important to New England and the proof was their relative value to the rest of the economy.

Edward Johnson's enumeration of 1651 reveals that at least 15 percent of all domestic animals in Massachusetts were sheep. In certain areas, such as Charlestown or Ipswich, the percentage was much higher with equal numbers of sheep and cattle grazing the town commons.[8] In Rhode Island and coastal Connecticut, the relative percentage of sheep to other livestock may even have been higher. Although not all families in Massachusetts owned sheep, all of them owned at least some wool, wool yarn or woolen clothing for their own use. Seventeenth-century probates reveal that in many households, cloth, cloth furnishings and clothing accounted for a substantial proportion of the household's wealth. Thus, the collective assets of the colony were influenced directly by domestic manufacture of woolens and, while divine providence may have helped to increase New England's flock, economic imperatives influenced colonial investment choices.

Even before Edward Johnson celebrated the size of New England's aggregate sheep flock, colonial legislatures expressed a deep interest in sheep. Urging that they be brought from England, a 1645 order from the Massachusetts Bay General Court read:

> . . . all ye towns in general and every one in particular within the jurisdiction, seriously to weigh the premises and accordingly that you will carefully endeavor the preservation and increase of such sheep as ye already have, as also to procure more . . . those such as have an opportunity to write to their friends in England . . . [and] advise them to bring as many sheep as conveniently they can . . . [9]

In this proclamation, the General Court acknowledged the damage done in England and in Europe by protracted wars that destroyed a large percentage of European flocks and made cloth expensive as well as difficult to obtain. Furthermore, although supply ships made regular visits to Massachusetts Bay, an adequate supply continued to be unpredictable. In the court's opinion, the absolute necessity for warm clothing in the cold and wet climate of New England made a home-based wool industry a necessity.

Restrictive legislation as well as official encouragement also characterized the Court's activities. At a session held on the 22nd of August 1654, the court set limits on slaughtering sheep for food and ordered a moratorium on the export sale of breeding animals. "No ramme or wether under two years can be butchered except by their owners until they reach two years . . . No person or persons shall transport any ewe or ewe lamb upon the forfeiture of five pounds each."[10]

By regulating the slaughter of rams and wethers less than two years old, the Court ensured the wool clip of two seasons before the animal was consumed.[11] Preserving rams past their first year also guaranteed at least one useful breeding season for that animal as well. Constraints placed upon the sale of the breeding ewes protected the fertility of the flock and prevented flock owners from succumbing to the high premiums paid for sheep in adjacent New England colonies as well as the mid-Atlantic region.[12] More to the point, such legislation prevented outsiders from siphoning off Massachusetts Bay's potential animal and wool production.

A similar trend can be found in the legislative efforts of Connecticut's General Assembly. In 1660, sheep were valued at 15 s. each for the purpose of "ye list of rates." Six years later, the Assembly took action again to promote the growth of sheep flocks when it exempted sheep from the list of rates making them an attractive asset. In addition, the Assembly required that tanners retain the ears of sheepskins when processed to prove ownership, prevent theft and confirm the proper age of the animal. Turning to management concerns, the Assembly established a formal provision for clearing suitable pasturage. By 1670, the Assembly emphasized the growth of Connecticut flocks when it confirmed the need for more sheep pasture and ordered every able-bodied male above the age of 14 to "work one day in the year sometime in June yearly" to speed the clearing of acreage.[13]

Some anticipated that their wool production could grow beyond meeting provincial needs and offer monetary enrichment: "[The Court] . . . having an eye to the good of posterity, . . . how profitable a merchandise it [woolen cloth] is likely to be, to transport to other parts [as staple trade items] . . . ."[14]

By 1699, this potentiality became evident when England reacted negatively to New England's expanding wool industry. Enacting restrictive legislation of their own, English lawmakers sought to remedy merchants' complaints that wool and woolen cloth produced in New England seriously affected their own market viability. Resolved that "no person may export in ships or carry by horses" to anywhere outside of their own colony "any wool or woolen manufactures of the English plantations in America," the English Board of Trade moved to prevent further colonial competition with England's manufacturers. The penalties were stiff. Any Americans who defied the order risked forfeiture of their ships and cargo as well as the payment of a £500 fine in English money.[15]

The threat to English woolen manufactures sprang from the enthusiasm with which colonists responded to the encouragement provided by the colonial governments of New England from 1645 onwards. In Massachusetts, probate inventories recorded in the period leading up to the 1699 order reveal the expansion of sheep ownership in the Bay Colony over the period.

In the first decade of settlement under study, only three probate inventories reported sheep in Essex and Suffolk Counties. After the 1645 appeal from the Massachusetts General Court, however, inventories reporting sheep multiplied. In the first decade after 1645, approximately 12 percent of all inventories reported sheep; between 1650 and 1690 more than one-third of all inventories contained them.

When the numbers for Essex and Suffolk Counties are examined more closely, Suffolk seems to experience a decline after mid-century, but this may be related to the fact that the town of Boston quickly became an urban hub and very different from the rest of the towns in the county. A considerable number of Boston's probate inventories after 1650 were those of single transient men; these were mostly sailors who tended to die young and with little personal property to distribute. The expansion of Boston as a seaport increased the number of young transient sailors and this distorts Suffolk County's overall rate. In addition, the rapid general growth of Boston restricted access to common pasture and this undoubtedly would have reduced opportunities for livestock ownership. As Edward Johnson commented, in just 14 years of settlement "Boston, the which of a poor country village, . . . is become like unto a small city."[16]

As a result, the number of Boston town inventories reporting sheep actually decreased over the period. Yet, when Boston's probates are extracted from Suffolk County's probates overall, the remaining towns show growth strikingly similar to Essex County's. Taken together, probate inventories recorded in the two counties indicate that sheep production began early in Massachusetts, especially north and west of Boston, and expanded at a fairly stable rate throughout the period. In this context, Johnson's 1651 estimate becomes a benchmark in the overall economic progress of the Bay colony.

Probate inventories in Connecticut and Plymouth Colony broadens that understanding. In Plymouth Colony probates available for the years 1633 to 1669, the number of inventories with sheep increased at a steady rate. In Plymouth Colony, wills and probate inventories recorded between 1633–1650 reveal eleven households that specifically listed sheep and several more listed "other cattel" beyond the oxen, calves and cows. Thus, 18 percent of Plymouth Colony households held sheep; this matches the situation in the Bay Colony. In the period from 1650 to 1669, Plymouth flocks expand to more than 20 percent of households. In the more prominent households flocks become larger; the inventories of William Bradford and Captain Myles Standish indicate they owned about 25 ewes, rams and lambs apiece. While the Plymouth Colony records do not extend beyond 1669, the trend towards larger flocks and more sheep seems clear.[17]

A small sample of probates taken from the colonial records of Connecticut indicates that the numbers of sheep reported are much the same as Massachusetts in the early years between 1639–50. Out of 46 inventories, seven report sheep. The repeated interest of the Connecticut Assembly after 1650 and their drive to provide more and better pasturage indicates that flocks were important and sheep were a familiar part of the farm landscape.

While the number of sheep on New England pastures generally indicates a successful husbandry, the numbers say little about strategies employed to manage or propagate them. Again, official documents provide some hints. The Massachusetts General Court issued regular proclamations covering pasture divisions and use as early as the 1630s. These chiefly directed all towns to allow liberal common usage for freemen developing sheep flocks. Between 1640 and 1645, the court also dispatched several orders encouraging sheep acquisition and propagation as well. Each order issued by the Court shared a common formula: each cited the essential nature of cloth to the continued success of the colony, the unreliable nature of imported sources and the economic hardship that imports placed on the immature economy.[18] Naturally, colonial legislative orders were implemented at the town level and it is there in various town selectmen records that local strategies can be observed:

> Whereas the [Massachusetts] General Court hath left it in the Selectmen of every Town to make orders for the clearing of their commons for the better keeping of their sheep.[19]

Thus, as a rule, selectmen of the town established the guidelines and allotments of common grazing, but always within the broad legislative recommendations of the Massachusetts Bay government. In this way, towns were able to add the particulars of their specific circumstances and needs while serving the larger interests of the colony. Indeed, all towns did not have the same access to common grazing land nor did every town have the same priorities.

In coastal towns, for instance, islands or small grassy peninsulas jutting into the sea offered perfect grazing areas that required little fencing or protection from predators. Likewise the animals were less likely to need fencing to protect meadows and crops. These areas were ideal, but by their very nature limited in capacity. After the first two decades, many coastal towns found themselves with grazing management problems as their herds and flocks multiplied. The minutes to the meetings of Ipswich (MA) selectmen (1634–1662) reveal the problems and solutions faced by one of the larger coastal towns' administration.

Although individuals owned sheep flocks, Ipswich sheep were usually pastured and managed as a single group for at least part of the year. Beginning in the 1630s, most of Ipswich common lands were made available for grazing from March to November. Very often, because their demand on the pasture grasses was far less stressful than that of the larger pasture animals, sheep were the first to move out to common pastures. Their small hooves and light body weights minimized potential danger to the sod, especially in the damp spring weather. In the fall, sheep were the last grazers brought in because they could glean sustenance from the dying fields longer than the larger foragers. In between, individuals kept flocks on their home lots, especially through the early spring lambing period.

Originally, Ipswich selectmen hired one or two herdsmen to take all of the town's livestock out to the commons each day between April and November. Sheep, goats and cows intermingled with little distinction made between the livestock species. All of the grazing animals had similar needs of water and grass meadows and, at first, a shared pasture made sense since one or two herdsmen could be hired to tend the entire town's "great Herd."

One can almost imagine William Fellows, the herdsman engaged by the town in January, 1639, moving from houselot to houselot collecting animals into the ungainly parade bound for Jeffries Neck, the first town common. In the misty morning just a half-hour after sunrise, Fellows would drive the animals out, perhaps with the help of his sons and maybe his dog. Once out on the Neck, Fellows closed the gate constructed by order of the town across the narrow strip of land connecting it to the mainland. Throughout the day, he guarded them against attack by stray dogs, wolves or other predators, but, more importantly, he prevented them from wandering back, pushing through the gate and laying waste to town gardens and fields. At the end of the day, "not before half an hour before sunset," the herd would retrace its steps, each animal probably turning eagerly in without prompting at the home gate.

For his pains, Fellows, and the other herdsmen who would be hired over the years, was paid in corn and grain, but also fined if the herd wandered and damaged property while under his care. Fellows, one of the town's sheep shearers, must have been a competent herdsman, since no fines associated with mismanagement was recorded in the Ipswich meetings through the period of his tenure.[20]

Under the watchful eye of William Fellows, the Ipswich livestock population quadrupled in less than 15 years. With such an enormous increase, the town's original common grazing land was no longer adequate and the selectmen began the process of dividing the "great herd." By 1654, the first common area, Jeffries Neck, was so over-grazed that only the sheep flock was allowed to pasture there. Four years later, the town subdivided the flock and hired the family of John Payne, living on Jeffries Neck, to provide a fold and care for half of the town's flock. Thomas Manning was contracted to put the rest on a new common cleared on the north side of the river.[21]

Under continued pressure from the expanding livestock population, selectmen worked to extend the town's pasturage and to regulate the commons already in use. Restricted from Jeffries Neck, cows, oxen, goats and horses needed additional pasture areas that could support their needs. In response, the selectmen decided to speed development of supplementary common pasture by requiring labor from each householder with a claim to common rights:

> Whereas . . . the Selectmen of this Town doth order that [of] the Inhabitants of this Town one able person of a family shall work one day in May or June as they shall be ordered according to the several divisions of the Town upon a days warning.[22]

Thus, the Ipswich selectmen worked to stay one step ahead of their prolific animal population.

Other regulations concerning common pasture usage limited individual townspeople's use. For example, a freeman who possessed a claim to common grazing was not able to put all of his animals willy-nilly out on the commons. Animals other than cows were regulated using a "cow standard" and were pastured accordingly: two horses to one cow, five sheep to one cow, and so on.[23] Each commonage right was measured by the number of cows it could accommodate and was clearly delineated by the holder's social and economic standing in the town's hierarchy. Proprietors enjoyed the best and largest portions of common rights, while freemen of inferior status were entitled to much less. Commonage rights most often accompanied the ownership of certain land divisions, but could be sold, leased, or devolved upon children independently.

A Rowley farmer, Francis Lambert, kept his "gates" and land together when he made his will in 1648.[24] Leaving the bulk of his estate to his eldest son, John, Lambert provided a small gift for his other sons out of the profits from their brother's share. The rest of the children received moveables and cash payments, but no land or common rights.[25] Nineteen years later, John Lambert died leaving his wife and two young children. Proved in 1667, Lambert's will assigned his father's commonages equally between his children, Abigail and John. Valued separately from the acreage, the common rights passed to the children as part of their inheritance. In this way, the "gates" became divorced, to a certain extent, from the original land divisions that assigned them to John's father, Francis Lambert.[26] With the death of her mother in 1681, Abigail Lambert was left homeless while still a minor. Heir to £4 of commonage in Rowley through her father, Abigail subsequently became the ward of her paternal uncle, Thomas. Ironically, Thomas Lambert, who did not inherit either land or common rights from his father, received at least temporary control over "rights of pasture" through his niece.[27]

Another Rowley family, the Stickneys, acquired additional common rights by leasing them. Entering into a lease agreement with the town in 1662, William and his son Samuel agreed to pay lease rent and to lay "dung" each year on land belonging to the church. Left to Rowley's church leadership by their first minister, Ezekiel Rogers, the land served to defray the cost of maintaining the ministry.[28] The new pasture increased the Stickney men's pasture holdings by at least eight acres, allowing them to expand the family's livestock holdings. Three years into the lease, William died leaving Samuel in control of the lease as well as his inherited commonages.[29]

For those who owned few animals, but more commonage rights, additional pasture privilege could be traded, sold or rented to another freeman with greater need, but only among town members. Animals from other towns were not often allowed pasture on the common land, even if sponsored by a resident.[30] Common grazing rights were carefully controlled within the town and protected against outside incursions.

The search for adequate pasture spawned many creative alternatives to meet individual farmers' needs. One industrious Ipswich freeman,

Robert Lord, capitalized on his position and the town's lack of pasture in an unusual way. Lord served his community in many capacities: as a selectman for the town of Ipswich in the 1650s, a clerk to the Essex County Quarterly Court, as a marshal and as the town grave digger. In 1650, he petitioned the Ipswich town meeting for control of the grass growing on the town burying ground. As gravedigger, Lord felt he had the greatest claim on that land and, subsequently, the town agreed. "As long as he continues to be employed in burying the dead," the grass was his to use or rent out as long as large animals such as cows or oxen were not trampling the graves of the departed citizens of Ipswich.[31]

The town of Marblehead experienced even more difficulties obtaining and developing adequate pasture partly because of geographic boundaries and partly because of poor quality pastures within the town. Located on a rocky coastal peninsula, Marblehead had limited grazing land available for its freemen from the beginning. By 1653, a group of Marblehead citizens claimed they were deprived of their fair share of common pasture. Town selectmen eventually agreed. However, since there was no additional common land to allocate them and no undeveloped land to improve, the selectmen agreed to purchase common rights on behalf of 44 families from a neighboring town.[32] In the same period only a few miles away, Salem town residents wrangled over restricted access to pasturage on Winter Island.[33]

For inland towns, the successful management of grazing animals hinged less on whether land could be developed and more on what land should be cleared and how it would be divided. Moreover, without the relative isolation of islands or areas like Jeffries Neck, livestock protection and control was more labor intensive in the interior towns. Fencing had to be erected around valuable meadows and crops while the animals, especially the larger flocks and herds had to be restrained. As we have seen, the Connecticut Assembly solved their need for sheep pastures by making it part of the general burden of work for citizens, much as they attended to the building of roads. The extra labor involved, then, promoted the proliferation of sheep in these areas. And, although the need for pasture did not stem solely from the growth of sheep flocks, the utility and versatility of the small animals made them popular. Indeed, according to one author of an early agricultural tract, sheep were used by inland towns to mend "poor land" by folding them on small areas where they consumed the briars, weeds and "mangy grass" making way for the growth of good English grass and other ruminants.[34] Due to the high nitrogen content of their manure, sheep provided vital nutrients for the soil, especially land devoted to growing grains.

A contemporary witness described in detail one town's use of their collective flock as a means to improve land:

23 December, 1704
[The people of Fairfield, Connecticut,] have an abundance of sheep,
whose very dung brings them great gain, with part of which they pay
their parson's sallery and they Grudge that, prefering their Dung before
their minister. They let out their sheep at so much as they agree upon
for a night; the highest bidder always carries them, and they [the sheep]
will sufficiently dung a large quantity of land before morning.[35]

Finding adequate pasturage was just one management difficulty faced
by livestock owners in Massachusetts towns by the 1650s. Another was
reproduction. Initially, the sheep flock—rams, wethers, adult ewes and
lambs—were kept together year round except for the period when individual flock owners held them on their homelots. As the size of the collective flocks grew, management of the pregnant ewes became more difficult.
Flock owners did not, for instance, know when their ewes had been bred
and therefore could not accurately predict lamb births. Lambing became
more erratic, losses became more frequent, and this created more difficulties
for individual farmers. When William Fellows had first watched over the
"great herd," he probably informed individual flock owners when breeding activity occurred, but once flocks began to number in the hundreds and
then in the thousands, such precise observation of ewe/ram mating was no
longer feasible. Again, the selectmen responded.

Beginning in 1659, Ipswich freemen voted to leave decisions concerning the sheep flock to the selectmen. Primary in their consideration
was the selectmen's goal of keeping rams from the ewes until "a con-
venient season."[36] Underlying this simple statement was the need of the
community to have control over the reproductive cycles of their animals.
Lambs born too early in the season risked freezing in the late winter cold
and those who survived had to be fed precious stocks of hay when weaned
before spring grass sprouted. Lambs born too late in the season were also
a problem since they continued to nurse their mothers after the time the
flocks should be culled and separated as well as ran greater risks of warm
weather disease and fly strike. Late lambs also prevented farmers from
an appropriate shearing time and disrupted the seasonal breeding cycle
by delaying ewes' lactation and estrus in the following season. By order-
ing the removal of the rams, the selectmen hoped to preserve a balance in
their flock's reproductive cycle and in the farmers' seasonal labor requirements as well.

A similar action was taken in Portsmouth when the "sheep-
men . . . moved in their town meeting" that they expected the town rams
to be put into the flocks at the proper time. Accordingly, they expected that

rams would not be put in with the flocks too soon—or withheld when they were needed.[37]

As we have seen, the collective sheep flock of Massachusetts Bay reached over 3,000 by 1650. Just 10 years later, the town of Ipswich managed upwards of a thousand. Similar growth occurred in Plymouth, Rhode Island and Connecticut towns, but the general growth of flocks does not tell us much about the individual sheep owners. How did an individual come to possess a part of this important resource? The obvious method was, of course, to follow the advice of the Massachusetts General Court order asking friends or relatives to bring them from England. However, it was not possible for every person who emigrated to bring livestock with them. Time resolved this issue, though, and, as flock sizes grew, opportunities for individuals to acquire breeding animals for their own use widened. One strategy for access to breeding animals and their wool can be found in the diary of Reverend Thomas Barnard of Salem.

Barnard acquired and developed a flock of his own through "renting" the sheep of another farmer, Simon Bradstreet. In 1687, Barnard entered into an agreement with Bradstreet to care for a small flock of eight ewes. The "rent" consisted of one-half of the flock's "increase" or half of all the lambs born to the flock each spring plus one for his table. Immediately after Barnard received the ewes, one died, but apparently Bradstreet did not consider the dead ewe a problem because the sheep stayed on at Barnard's. Between 1687 and 1692, Barnard carefully noted in his journal each year's lamb crop, the number of sheep he killed for mutton and any other deaths. At the end of six years, Barnard now owned 10 adult ewes of his own. In the spring of 1692, he delivered 12 ewes, the 7 original ewes and 5 of the "increase," to his neighbor, John Farnum, who became Bradstreet's new sheep tenant.

Continuing to record his flock's activity, Barnard reckoned each year's increase in lambs. He likewise tallied slaughtered sheep for his table as well as wolf depredations.[38] On average, Barnard kept about 10 breeding ewes, 6 wethers, a ram or two, and consumed 2 lambs each year. By 1707, his flock size leveled out at about 30. One can only guess if John Farnum enjoyed as much success as Reverend Barnard, but given the regular increase in the numbers of sheep reported in probate inventories over the period, it seems likely.[39]

A reliable investment, flocks became regular features in probate documents as part of the proposed legacies for widows and children. Often used as a moveable inheritance, men made bequests of as few as one or as many as several hundred in their wills. For instance, Myles Standish left five sheep in his will to his son Josiah. A younger son, this was presumably a "seed" flock from which he could develop a future income.[40] Another example of this strategy is evident in the will of Hugh Alley, a lesser farmer from Lynn. Alley judiciously divided his small flock of 12 sheep amongst his family:

> This 2 day of the 11 month 1673 . . . the last will of hugh ally Sener I give to my son John Ally a yew sheep and lamb at mickelmas next his wife and children for to have the yuse of them tele the children com to age and then the children to have the yew shep and the lamb and the incres of these sheep, I give to my grandchild John linsy at michalmase next a ewe shep and the first ewe lamb that this ewe brings his brother Elizer linsy shall have . . . [41]

Under the terms of his will, Alley gave each of his children and grand-children a ewe and the first ewe-lamb born to it. The rest of the flock, about five, became the property of his wife, Mary Alley, to dispose of as she "sese most nede." It seems likely that Alley's flock remained intact despite its diverse ownership pattern, except perhaps when individual animals were sold or slaughtered. Indeed, the communal nature of most towns' approach to flock management made it possible for people like Hugh Alley to own a few sheep, but still manage to propagate enough animals to provide children with a small inheritance of a few animals apiece.

The account book kept by Topsfield weaver John Gould illustrates the diverse ownership possible in an Essex County flock. Keeping track of his share of the wool and lamb crop, Gould noted in 1698 that there were 85 animals in the flock that included his own. His father, two brothers, Goodman Bixby and Goodwife Cary all owned a portion of the flock, which was serviced by a neighbor's ram. The ewes, wethers and lambs all foraged together and were identified by tattoos or distinguishing marks made on their ears at spring shearing time. The group shared the cost of pasture for their flock and carefully separated the wool crop at shearing time.[42] Goodwife Cary, as Mary Alley may have done, benefited from her association with the Goulds and Goodman Bixby in the reduced cost of maintaining her small flock.

Probate evidence supports the view that sheep, as an easily kept and potentially abundant animal, was useful for people of limited means like Hugh and Mary Alley.

Chart 1. Wealth Distribution of Probates Reporting Sheep in the Period 1630–1690.

Colony	£0–200	£201–500	£501–800	£801+	Total
Mass Bay	193–42%	158–34%	64–14%	49–10%	464–100%
Plymouth	20–65%	8–26%	1–3%	2–6%	31–100%
Connecticut	4–24%	9–52%	2–12%	2–12%	17–100%

In the chart above, the largest percentage of probates reporting sheep were those valued less than £200 and almost half of all inventories recorded in the period fell in the same category. The prevalence of sheep in the probate records of the "lower sort" such as Hugh Alley points to several factors: sheep were relatively inexpensive to maintain compared to cows, were more prolific as they often twinned, and readily available.

These factors were reflected in the lower price of sheep over the period. In 1645, the average cost of a yearling ewe was 40 shillings. This relatively high valuation suggests a limited supply and a large demand. By 1660, prime bloodstock brought one-quarter the price, 10 shillings, making the purchase of six sheep equal to the purchase of one cow. Fifteen years later, the average price halved to five shillings verifying that the supply of animals grew well enough to meet the demand over the period. As sheep became more prevalent, they became more affordable for poorer farmers in general.[43]

In practical terms, sheep were ideal for people who had less access to grazing. They could subsist on inferior, even meager, amounts of forage compared to the needs of cattle. As we have seen, sheep cost less per animal, and, because of their relatively small size, required less space. Moreover, their reproductive patterns allowed farmers to increase the size of a flock readily.

Gestation for sheep lasted five months, half that of a cow. One season's pregnancy usually terminated in at least two offspring and sometimes three compared to the bovine birth pattern of a single calf. Moreover, once they were born, lambs matured at a much faster rate than calves, reaching sexual maturity by five to six months. Calves, on the other hand, took 18 months to two years to reach reproductive age. Finally, because a ewe lamb could be bred in the first year, the flock reproduced geometrically each year. All of these factors combined made the return on a venture such as Reverend Barnard's far less risky than if he "rented" cows. In this way, sheep can be seen as the best poor man's livestock.

Yet, the bulk of sheep were not owned by the "lower sort" of people. Instead, as the table below demonstrates, the average flock size grew in proportion to the value of the probate, especially in Massachusetts. For all the same reasons that sheep might appeal to a farmer of limited reserves and means, they appealed to more prosperous colonists as well.

Chart 2. Average Flock Size Related to Probate Value

Colony	£0–200	£201–500	£501–800	£801+
Mass Bay	8	15	22	45
Plymouth	7	12	14	14
Connecticut	8	11	16	25

Chart 3. Number of Probate Inventories Reporting Wool Fiber

Year	Bay Colony	Plymouth	Connecticut
1630–49	62/189—33%	6/37—16%	9/46—20%
1650–69	141/1029—14%	48/130—37%	4/16—25%
1670–89	293/1302–23%	n/a	5/ 18—28%

A more prosperous farmer, such as Simon Bradstreet, might own as many as 200 sheep, but in arrangements with lesser men, he could "rent" out his entire flock in small groups. In this manner, Bradstreet could tap into a greater share of the town common grazing lands and labor market without investing more than the cost of his flock. Each time his flock reproduced, he was guaranteed a share of the new lambs, their fleeces, and paid out only half of the "profit" to his tenants. Unless the sheep flock suffered enormous damage from wolves or disease, its continued growth in size and value was as certain as each new spring crop of lambs and wool.

As the Massachusetts General Court outlined in its 1645 order, it was the wool that made sheep most appealing to New England colonists. Easily processed into cloth, wool was warmth and survival in the winter and possibly a trade product as well. Probate inventories indicate the presence of raw wool in a significant numbers.

The average yield from a "good" English sheep breed in this period was approximately four to six pounds per year. This meant that a person who kept only two or three sheep could expect to harvest between eight and 18 pounds at shearing time. Once the housewife processed her wool, she could have as much as five or six pounds of finished yarn, certainly enough for five or six yards of cloth. For larger flocks, the yield was much greater and could produce impressive amounts of marketable wool. As we have seen, by mid-century the collective flock of the north shore of Massachusetts had the potential to produce a substantial volume of raw wool each year, the 1651 wool crop amounting to over six tons. In Rhode Island, the 1654 estimate of thousands indicates that it could equal if not surpass Massachusetts' production.

At first glance, the acquisition and propagation of sheep in early New England appears to have been exclusively a male concern. From the broadest legislation enacted by the members of the Massachusetts General Court down to less lofty discussions between selectmen over the pasturing and breeding cycles of their flocks, men presided over every detail. However, closer examination reveals that women invested more than a passing interest and involvement in this seemingly male-dominated arena.

Spring lambing, for instance, was clearly a time when women, rather than men, were most involved with the sheep. Kept in a "barth" built near or in the house yard, pregnant ewes were carefully watched for signs of delivery. In most cases, lambing probably went smoothly, but often enough a ewe needed human help to birth a particularly large or unusually laid lamb. Since children and their housework held them in place, women were more likely to have kept "lambing vigils" over their families' flocks. Moreover, as the recent work of women's historians has shown, women have traditionally been responsible for the milch cows, chickens and bacon pigs kept close to the house.[44]

Other factors indicate women's involvement as well. Given the relatively small size of ewes and their vaginas, as well as their propensity to birth twins, a woman's smaller hands and general knowledge of midwifery made her more likely to care for the ewes during this time. Once lambs were born, lactating ewes sometimes produced more milk than their lambs could consume and this abundance could make them ill if they consumed too much. The remedy was to milk ewes out, at times twice a day, and this undoubtedly fit in with the regular routine of milking the family milch cow. The extra milk was very often used to make an especially rich cheese or mixed with the cow's milk for a higher protein ratio. An English verse elucidates this bonus of extra milk from the flock:

> To milk and to fold them, is much to require,
> Except we have pasture to fill their desire.
> Yet many by milking (such heed do they take),
> Not hurting their bodies, much profit they take.
> Five ewes to a cow, make a proof by a score,
> Shall double thy dairy, or trust me no more,
> Yet may a good housewife that knoweth the skill,
> Have mixt or unmixt, at her pleasure and will.[45]

The opposite problem—too little milk—could also occur and then lambs had to be sorted out, fed manually or grafted onto ewes that could support the extra lamb. Lambs required watching, too. Gelded and docked soon after they were born, new lambs needed to be coddled for a few days before they regained strength and growth.[46]

The bulk of these chores fell solidly within the realm of the nurturing role that women expected to fulfill and, most likely, did. In the early spring of the year when the days were still short and the garden chores still a month or two away, it is easy to imagine Mary Alley keeping a lambing vigil. Lighting an early-morning lantern, wrapping up in a shawl and trudging out to the sheep pen, Mary Alley would check the ewes' progress. Amid the cacophony of lamb bawls and ewe grunts, she would look for signs of imminent birth, feel the bellies of the newborn lambs for warmth and fullness and perhaps throw a few dried apples to her favorite ewes.

By the end of March, lambs were weaned and then ewes, wethers and rams were re-assembled and washed. Washing them merely removed the outer dirt and vegetable fibers that collected in their coats over the winter months and made shearing them less difficult. Generally this was done in a millpond or a sluggish stream (a strong current would carry the animals away and drown them) and usually when the weather had warmed sufficiently for them to dry off quickly in the sun. A few days later, they would be sheared and, even then, women played an important part.

Thomas Tusser described the obvious female contribution to this event best; his verse indicates a tradition of community-based sheep management that harked back to England in the previous century:

> Wife, make us a dinner, spare flesh neither corn,
> Make wafers and cakes, for our sheep must be shorn.
> At sheep-shearing, neighbors none other thing crave,
> But good cheer and welcome, like neighbors to have.[47]

Aside from providing meals for the nourishment of the men like William Fellows of Ipswich who wrestled, caught and sheared the flock, women performed other tasks as well. Some women probably sheared. In England, it was not uncommon for a woman to be a "clipper of sheepe." An account book held in the Sussex Archaeological Collections recorded payment to "the wife of Geo. Baker for shearing 23 sheep." Another from Norfolk assessed a woman shearer's wages.[48] In New England, evidence of shearing arrangements remains unclear. William Fellows certainly owned sheep shears; they were in his probate inventory and, as a town shepherd, it seems likely he knew how to use them, but it could easily have been his wife that wielded them come shearing time.

Shearing day was most likely chosen and organized by town selectmen, but women and children certainly joined in the process. As the shearers cut each fleece away from the body of the sheep, helpers laid the fleeces out and "skirted" them. Skirting was the process of removing all of the manure tags and urine-soaked wool sheared near the rump, head and belly of the sheep. Leaving the soiled portions on would ruin the rest of the fleece if left together. The tag ends, belly wool and soiled pieces skirted from the fleece were then soaked clean in a tub with soapy water and then laid out to dry in the shade. Later, housewives used this lower quality fiber for felting or for stuffing comforters or cushions. These tag ends may also have been the only source of wool for the truly poor who had less access to animal products.[49] Once fleeces were skirted, helpers rolled them up with the skin side facing out, tied them into small bundles and carried them away to dry attics until further processing. All of these tasks required minimal physical strength and tended to be seen as appropriate work for women and children.

Once lambs were weaned and shearing done, the flocks generally began their early summer grazing cycle and returned to the care of the town shepherds. Even then, it is possible that men and women shared responsibility for protecting or watching over the sheep. In mid-seventeenth century England, one woman wrote that when she walked on the common land close to her home, she encountered "a great many young wenches" who kept sheep and cows.[50] With so many of England's customs re-created in New England, it seems likely that young women in Massachusetts could have done similar work. Moreover, since shared work was by custom credited to the head of household, the wives' and children's participation was nearly always obscure except to contemporaries. A case in point was John Payne of Ipswich.

Appointed shepherd for a portion of Ipswich's flock in 1658, Payne became one of William Fellow's successors. His share of the flock, approximately four hundred animals, was to be folded on his farm with provisions for pasture being made both on Jeffries Neck as well as on his own farm lot. The contract between Payne and the town specified that he "fold them upon his farm" for one half of the year and the common for the other.[51] One would assume that it was he who watched and guarded the sheep, but Payne was a sailor, possibly a fisherman, who frequently went to sea. Who was did the shepherding chores in his absence? As recent studies of colonial labor patterns have shown, New Englanders relied heavily on "native-born family" for their labor needs. With this in mind, Payne's wife and children seem likely candidates.[52]

Whether wives and children worked with the flock prior to the harvest of wool probably varied as much as the number of families who owned sheep, but once the wool clip came home their labor was indispensable. Stored in the attics and lofts of their homes until winter, wool became the post-harvest focus of most households and children were very often set to the task of opening the fleece bundles, sorting and picking the wool.

When sorting, children may have separated the different lengths and quality of fibers that came from each individual animal's body. The most desirable part of the fleece, the back and shoulder wool, was pulled out and set aside as the "top." These were the longest and usually the softest fibers in the whole fleece. The head, belly and leg wool was set aside as inferior wool that could be used for stuffing comforters or mattresses, while the remainder was set aside for felt making.[53]

Once the fleeces were sorted (or sometimes while they were in the process), they would be picked clean of hay seeds, burdocks and other vegetable matter the sheep gathered in its fleece while browsing in open pastures over the course of the year. Pickers worked mainly by simply pulling the fibers apart and shaking the plant debris loose, but more ambitious households may have used a mechanical wool picker. A hand-powered machine, the mechanical picker swung back and forth in a pendulum motion over long teeth that helped to pull wool fibers apart and release plant matter from its tangle.

The next step in preparing wool for spinning was the carding process. Children were often chosen for this activity because its easy and repetitious nature required little supervision. Using two wooden paddles studded with nails or thin wires or fitted with dried teasles, a carder combed the wool by passing the rough surfaces of the hand cards across each other until the wool fibers were all lying in the same direction. Combed wool was peeled carefully off the hand cards and rolled into tube-like structures, which were stacked in baskets to be spun later.

Spinning was so exclusively a female activity that the word "spinster" became synonymous with an unmarried woman, perhaps at first because it was mainly unmarried daughters who worked at their mother's or neighbors' spinning wheels before their marriage. Spinning occurred in a variety of settings. Women with wheels could spin their own or a neighbor's fiber. Easily interrupted, housewives could spin in between the demands of caring for small children or ailing relatives. Unmarried women could spin to earn extra money or fulfill a debt of labor owed to another household. Since spinning was not physically demanding, elderly women could contribute to a family's workload without the physical stress of digging vegetables or milking the family cow.

Spun yarn was most likely used as soon as it was manufactured, but some families kept stocks of yarn as surplus produce or in anticipation of a market demand. Evidence of household yarn stocks can be detected in the probate records of the period.

Chart 4. Number of Probate Inventories Reporting Wool Yarn by Probate Value, 1630–1690.

Probate Value	Bay Colony	Plymouth	Connecticut
£0–200	80/1270—6%	31/140—22%	8/45—18%
£201–500	89/532—17%	5/24—21%	5/26—19%
£501–800	29/153—19%	2/3—60%	1/5—20%
£800+	26/132—20%	0 / 0	1/6—17%

As Chart 4 demonstrates, the poorer households of the Bay Colony tended to keep yarns less frequently, while the wealthier homes were more likely to keep them. This likely reflects a market strategy where households with greater access to wool used their skills and tools to produce materials bound for market as well as for their own consumption. Although the samples are much smaller in Plymouth and Connecticut, there seemed to be a tendency for less range in how yarn stocks were held. Perhaps because there was less range in wealth in the samples, the tendencies in the Massachusetts sample are not detectable. Frequency of appearance in probates, however, cannot tell the whole story. The volume of wool yarn held can also be instructive. The Massachusetts Bay sample provides some evidence that different geographic areas employed different strategies when stockpiling yarns.

As Chart 5 shows, Essex County households with higher probate values stored more wool yarn while in Suffolk County the yarn was not concentrated in one economic sector. Rather, the distribution of yarn stocks may indicate that in Suffolk County, yarn may have been much less important as a market product. This is not to say that Suffolk County had less yarn production, rather to suggest that the products made from yarn may have been more lucrative. Another possibility could be that Suffolk County spinners did not own the wool they spun and passed the finished yarn off as soon as it was processed.

Spun wool was utilized in two major ways: knitted garments or woven cloth. Knitted garments included such items as stockings, scarves, shawls, sweaters and mittens. George Curwin, a seventeenth-century Salem merchant, credited a number of accounts for stocking knitting and, in turn, sold three dozen pairs of stockings to regular customers between 1652 and 1655.[54] Clearly these items came to Curwin from men whose wives, daughters or employees plied their needles and used the result to satisfy their debt with the merchant.

In his daybook between sheep flock tallies, Rev. Thomas Barnard recorded regular employment of the daughters of his neighbor and fellow

Chart 5. Volume of Wool Yarn Reported in Bay Colony Probate Inventories, 1630–1690

Probate Value	Essex County	Suffolk County
£ 0–200	643# (16# av.)	515# (13# av.)
£201–500	1080# (37# av.)	583# (10# av.)
£501–800	664# (83# av.)	285# (14# av.)
£800+	624# (57# av.)	64# (4# av.)

sheep owner, John Farnum. As we have seen, Mary and Betsey Farnum did a number of tasks for Barnard including spinning, knitting and bleaching linen. Barnard recorded each transaction and credited the wages paid accordingly. In November of 1693, the sisters received 12 shillings for their knitting, perhaps even knitting stockings meant for a merchant like George Curwin.[55]

Still another reference to knitting as a means of female employment is found in the story of Mary Rowlandson, captured by Indians in a Narraganset raid on her Lancaster, Massachusetts, home in 1676. Finding it difficult to survive on the traveling rations provided by her captors, Rowlandson used her knitting skills to bargain for extra food. The most frequently mentioned item was stockings. The yarn she used to knit came mainly from picked-apart stockings, items routinely stolen in raids on Massachusetts' farmsteads.[56]

Although knitting fulfilled important needs in colonial households, making woven cloth was the primary purpose of spun wool, and spinners were kept busy producing yarn bound for the loom. On average, one weaver could keep 20 full-time spinners busy, although in practice a weaver probably worked sporadically as yarn came in from specific households. Woolen cloth came in a variety of weights and weaves depending on its use. The most common types of wool cloth were broadcloth, serge and kersey.[57]

Weavers, both professional and vernacular, manufactured broadcloth with a plain or "tabby" weave. Produced on a large loom, broadcloth tended to be more than twice the usual width of woven cloth, between 54 and 63 inches, and a standard length of 24 yards. Hard wearing, thick-textured and warm, broadcloth made ideal outer clothing, especially in the colder months of the year. Yarn destined to become broadcloth was always carded before spinning, creating a "worsted" yarn, and sometimes dyed as well. Once woven, broadcloth was not properly finished until it was fulled, a process that felted, tightened and thickened the fabric.[58] Rowley weavers, drawing on their Yorkshire roots, continued to produce broadcloth in Essex County; they were the first in New England to build a fulling mill. The entire process tended to make broadcloth the most expensive of the provincial wool fabrics produced in this period, making it a profitable, but limited market product. Other cheaper types of wool cloth were produced to fit the needs of poorer households.

Serge was considered a lesser quality than broadcloth. Narrower and produced with less finishing, serge served an important role in the middling to lower colonial households. A twill weave, serge fabric was mid-weight rather than heavy and cheaper since the finishing process was far less labor intensive than that of broadcloth. Used as an all-purpose fabric, serge could become upholstery, bed curtains, blankets and, for those who could not

Chart 6. Number of Inventories Reporting New Wool Cloth, 1630–1690

Probate Value	Mass Bay	Plymouth	Connecticut
£ 0–200	114/1270—9%	55/140—39%	9/45—20%
£201–500	73/532—14%	13/24—54%	10/26—39%
£501–800	16/153—11%	2/3—66%	2/5—40%
£801+	14/132—11%	0 / 0	2/4—50%

afford broadcloth, clothing. Notifying the English Council on Trade in 1705, Lord Cornbury, Governor of the Province of New York cautioned the Council to disrupt the production of serge in New England. "I myself have seen serge . . . [produced there that] any man may wear," he wrote. Pointing out that production of cloth in New England and other English colonies bred independence in America and trouble for English merchants in London, Cornbury called for an immediate suspension of colonial textile manufacture.[59]

The least expensive pure woolen cloth was kersey. A twill weave made from the roughest of yarn, kersey was seldom fulled and only poorly dyed. As a result, kersey fit a wide range of uses similar to that of serge, but could be produced quite inexpensively and sold very cheap. The low cost made it available to the poor who regarded kersey as an all-purpose fabric.

All three types of locally produced woolens found their way into New England's households and probate inventories confirm their existence.

At first glance, the percentage of probates reporting new wool cloth in Massachusetts Bay over the period seems low. However, when one views these stocks as available *after* the clothing or other wool cloth needs were met, the numbers become more significant. The samples for Plymouth and Connecticut are smaller and the numbers for Plymouth Colony do not cover the whole period, but the evidence suggests that a considerable volume of woolen cloth was available from local weavers. Another way to evaluate the samples is to combine them. These inventories indicate that more than 13 percent of all New England households recorded in probate inventories held surplus fabric in reserve.

Clearly, by the end of the century, provincial manufacture of wool cloth reached levels that made the "comfortable living" desired by the Massachusetts General Court in 1645 possible. The "miracle" of sheep and wool production observed by Edward Johnson in 1654 was even more evident. However, such abundance was less the result of divine intervention as it was the result of traditional practices and suitable conditions. Following labor customs established long before their emigration, New Englanders developed their sheep flocks by careful management and hard work. The wool crop harvested from their flocks provided an ever-increasing resource from which the domestic cloth would be manufactured. Woolen cloth produced in New England filled a gap made by the distance to England and the debt associated with colonial settlement. By the 1690s, the long-term goal set by the colonial governing bodies of an exportable staple wool crop must have seemed imminent. One observer claimed that over three-fourths of all textiles used in New England were locally produced.[60] However, whether or not the provincial cloth industry seriously challenged English textiles abroad, the potential benefits anticipated in 1645 were certainly fulfilled in the towns and villages of Massachusetts.

Chapter Two
Flax from the Field, Cotton from the Sea

"hemp and flax here [in New England] is [in] great plenty"
—Captain Edward Johnson, 1642[1]

If seventeenth-century New Englanders only raised sheep and produced woolen cloth, they would have engaged in a significant textile industry that employed many hands, covered much of the colonists' nakedness and made economic success possible. Yet sheep and wool composed only a portion of early New England's textile efforts. Equal to the woolen industry in scope was the growth and processing of flax and hemp and the production of provincial linen and cotton fabrics. As one contemporary noted, "In [New England's] prospering hemp and flax so well that its frequently sown, spun, and woven into linen cloth; . . . and our linen yarn we can make dimittees and fustians for our summer clothing."[2]

Just as wool was manufactured into different fabrics, linen came in many weights and weaves. Under the rubric of "linen," household fabrics ranged widely in quality and use. Loosely woven strainer or cheesecloth differed little in fiber content from the fabric that became pudding bags or flour sacking.[3] Linen yarn woven in a diaper weave became table linen or toweling. Other linen yarns could be woven into sheets, pillow covers, or aprons while the same yarns could be sent to the fancy weaver to be fashioned into more valuable tablecloths or napkins. Tow yarns, woven densely, became sail canvases, bed ticking or mattress covers.

As the author of *New England's First Fruits* observed, linen was also an important fabric for certain types of clothing, mainly the clothing worn closest to the skin. In a typical seventeenth-century inventory, men's shirts, women's shifts and other sorts of "wearing linging" were undoubtedly linen cloth. Given its homely nature, most of that fabric was undoubtedly locally grown and processed. Whether left natural or "brown" in color, dyed or bleached white after weaving, linen was used in a range of basic clothing from underwear to heavy canvas garments.[4] However, some fabrics were actually "mixed" cloth made up of domestic linen warp and imported cotton wefts.

New England obtained cotton from the West Indies along with the more oft-cited cargo of molasses. Historians have repeatedly told the story of how ingenious Yankees turned West Indian molasses into gallons of exported rum. While dreaming of rum, these same historians have totally ignored the importation of cotton and how New England men and women manufactured mountains of domestically-consumed cloth.

Cotton had been recently taken up as a textile fiber in England, but once adopted it rapidly become popular. In less than 30 years after its introduction into mainstream English fabrics, cotton became an important ingredient for constructing better, more comfortable clothing.

> About twenty yeeres past [ca. 1602] diverse people in this Kingdome,
> but chiefly in the County of Lancaster, have found out the trade of
> making of other [cloth] . . . ,made of a kind of Bombast or Downe,
> being a fruit of the earth growing upon little shrubs or bushes, brought
> into this Kingdome . . . , but commonly called cotton Wooll.[5]

The "cotton wooll," a sea island variety with long staples, landed in New England from English plantations on the islands of the West Indies, especially Barbados. John Winthrop summed up the situation in a 1647 journal entry:

> As our means of returns for English commodities was grown very short,
> it pleased the Lord to open us a trade with Barbados and other Islands
> in the West Indies, which as it proved gainful, so the commodities we
> had in exchange there for our cattle and provisions, as sugar, cotton,
> tobacco, and indigo were a good help to discharge our engagements to
> England.[6]

New England colonists interested in developing domestic textiles traded for Barbadian cotton as early as 1635 because they knew the utility and value of cotton/linen fabrics. Such fabric was durable, absorbent and easily washed. Fustians and dimities were the most common types manufactured and fit a wide range of uses.

Fustians, a large group of general-purpose fabrics were mainly woven with a tight heavy texture. Sometimes they were plainly woven, but fustians could also be fashioned with "tufts" creating fabric like corduroy or velveteen. Fustians were used for anything from draperies to dresses or upholstery to men's waistcoats. Generally, though, it served as extremely durable outerwear fabrics, especially in the summer months when hot weather made heavy worsted wool outerwear unbearable.[7]

Dimities were a self-patterned fabric that could be coarse or more finely woven fabric, very often decorated. One 1696 draper's handbook held that dimities of the finer type were best used to "line breeches" and "foot stokings" or for men's waistcoats and women's petticoats.

Cotton was also used in a plain weave with a linen warp to produce "mixed cloth." This could be made into undergarments, or "small clothes," shifts, chemises and drawers; all could be easily rinsed out and dried, even in the winter months. The softer hand of the fabric made wearing heavy woolen twill fabrics, especially those not fulled properly, bearable.[8]

As a popular fiber in the colonies, cotton was deemed so important that provincial committees of trade were routinely directed to acquire an adequate supply for their town. A decree issued by the General Assembly of Connecticut in 1641 is instructive,

> Whereas yt ys thought necessary for the comfortable support of these plantations that a trade in cotton wooll be set upon and attempted and for furthering thereof, yt hath pleased the Governor, that now is, to undertake the furnishing and setting forth a vessell with convenient speed to those parts where the said commodity is to be had, yf yt prove phesable.[9]

The Connecticut governor subsequently commissioned the ship that returned 18 months later with a cargo amounting to approximately 12,000 pounds of "cotton wooll." The cotton bales were then divided among the towns and sub-divided among the freeholders who were willing to pay the "rate" set to finance the voyage. Similar ventures were underwritten by Massachusetts towns.

The steady traffic of Caribbean cotton can be seen in a variety of extant seventeenth-century records. One source is the probate records of New England merchants. Mahalaleel Munnings, a Boston merchant with overseas connections, is a case in point. An inventory of his warehouse made upon his death in 1659 revealed a shipment of nine bags of raw cotton weighing close to a ton. Judging from his outstanding accounts, Munnings apparently speculated on the sale of these goods; most were designated in the account as the property of an overseas source.[10] His investment in West Indian cotton was not unique.

George Curwin, a prosperous Salem merchant, had overseas connections that regularly brought in West Indian products, especially cotton. In three account books spanning the years 1652 to 1662, Curwin recorded the dispersal of raw cotton to his customers almost daily. Over the course of 10 years, the more complete of the volumes reveal that Curwen sold at least two and maybe three bags of raw cotton each year, roughly 600 to 800 pounds. In a similar ledger where he noted cargo brought in from the West Indies by his own ships, Curwin tallied a total of over a ton of cotton received in two seasons' voyages.[11] When Curwin died in 1681, his estate inventory included three bags stored in his warehouse.[12]

About half of the cotton that arrived on Curwin's wharf in Salem was the property of Barbadian planters who shipped the cotton for credit to be paid in New England's most available currency: salted meat and fish, grains, rum or forest products. Barbadian planters were well aware that cotton could be sold as easily as sugar in the New England ports, especially Providence, Salem and Boston. Upon his arrival in Salem harbor, Francis Ellis, a merchant mariner, notified his Barbadian clients of the state of the market:

> I doubt the sale of goods will be slow, I understand that rum is in at 3s, . . . cotton at the most 18d and doubt it will fall to 16d. . . . yet shall we use all dilligence to make a sale for your best advantage . . . I hope to carry the return items myself.[13]

The diligence referred to by Ellis was not so much his need to rush about selling his cargo as his efforts to land the cargo in Salem. The harbormaster refused to allow his cargo to be landed for fear of summer "pestilence" accompanying Ellis' sailors to shore. In several angry letters Ellis badgered the port authorities to allow him to dock, claiming that his ship was healthier than the streets of Salem. Three days after Ellis' protest letters, the cargo was landed and the cotton sold for a good price.[14]

Between 1688 and 1692 Samuel Ingersol, a Salem mariner, recorded the shipping fees for a total of more than 16 bags of cotton in his daybook. Over half was the property of a Barbadian planter known only as "Mr. Jardin," while a few bags may have been his own investment. Ingersol regularly acted for at least four different merchant/growers in Barbados. As agent, he frequently carried cloth back from Salem as payment for the raw cotton.[15]

Salem merchants well understood the value of imported cotton as a likely commodity for investment. Aboard the ship, *Prudent Mary*, as its new master in March of 1694, Samuel Ingersol received instructions for

William Gedney's outbound cargo through Joseph Grow, master of a ship bound for New Foundland. Apparently, Gedney knew Grow would meet Ingersol's ship to exchange some of the rum shipped from Salem for part of the salted fish bound for Barbados.

> Memorandum. Mr. Joseph Grow.
>
> Please to ship the effects of my two hogsheads of fish [got in exchange for two of rum] in good raw cotton with Mr. Samuel Ingersol if he comes for New England.
>
> William Gedney

In a routine already well established for nearly a decade, Ingersol loaded four full bags and one partially full of cotton at Barbados for the return voyage to Salem.[16]

Tristrum Hull of Barnstable in Plymouth Colony also traded in cotton. His ship, the bark *Hopewell*, engaged in the coastal trade and may well have sailed to the West Indies. In the inventory taken at his death in 1666, he held over 150 pounds of cotton in a warehouse next to wine, rum, sugar and beaver pelts. His extensive estate also included fabrics, many made of cotton and cotton blended with linen and wool. Although some of the fabrics in his inventory were probably imported, it is also easy to imagine that Blanche Hull may have spun cotton on the wheel reported in the probate inventory.[17]

Not everyone who wished to import West Indian cotton was a blue water merchant or otherwise connected to the rum trade. Anyone willing to risk the "bold venture" of Atlantic sea-trade could take a chance. A friend of Samuel Barton's decided to gamble on his horse. In a letter to Samuel Taylor, a Barbadian merchant, Barton outlined what his friend intended,

> Sir, the enclosed is a bill of lading for one dark bay stone horse about four years old. Ship [the horse] to friend Joseph Pope on board the Brigantine Newberry, Ralph Lindsay, Master, for Barbados which he desires you would sell for him to his best advantage and the meet proceeds to send to him at first opportunity for Salem in good rum and cotton woole.[18]

Although the reverse side of Barton's missive shows notations regarding the cost of the horse's transport and feed, no corresponding memorandum survives of the rum and cotton proceeds from the sale of the horse. However, it is not difficult to imagine what Barton's friend did with his return cargo. Cotton would have provided him with a currency of sorts, mostly in the form of credit with a merchant. He could also have directly used the cotton or traded it for something he wanted more. This is exactly what Robert Barker did when he bought ten acres of land from Edward Hunt and paid mostly in "cotton woole."[19] For many farmsteads in New England, though, cotton became available through the merchants who supplied their other market needs.

Scattered throughout seventeenth-century account books, miscellaneous papers and daybooks kept by farmers and small merchants are the lesser transactions that mark the movement of cotton into the homes of textile producers. Joshua Buffum, a small Salem merchant, routinely debited cotton wool, generally between 10 and 20 pounds, to his customers' accounts. In addition, he sometimes credited accounts with cotton thread presented as payment. One such account, Josia Wollcott's, reveals an active textile-manufacturing household that produced a total of several hundred pounds of spun thread and 85 yards of woven fabric in the years between 1688 and 1700. Interspersed with Wollcott's purchases of sugar and other household staples were the pounds of raw cotton that returned, in part, as either spun thread or woven cloth to Buffum's establishment.[20]

George Curwin's 1655–1657 ledgers debited a variety of customers for regular purchases of "cotton wool." Analysis of his customer accounts over the course of three years reveals a clear pattern. Most households purchased an average of 20 pounds of cotton each year, usually in just one transaction per year. Virtually all purchases occurred in the winter months after harvest and before spring planting in a time when textile activity may well have been most active. Lastly, the same households tended to purchase their cotton at nearly identical times of the year, some preferring late fall and others early spring. This regularity of purchase suggests that the cycle of farm chores and seasons also influenced the household production of textiles even when the fibers utilized were available throughout the year.[21]

As we can see from the Wollcott family and George Curwin's clientele, the regular flow of West Indian cotton into New England ports made it possible for textile producing households to obtain raw cotton whenever they required.

Chart 7. Number of Probates Reporting Cotton Fiber

Year	Bay Colony	Plymouth	Connecticut
1630–49	6/189—3%	4/37—11%	7/46—15%
1650–69	79/1029—8%	32/130—25%	2/16—13%
1670–89	129/1302—10%	n/a	1/18—6%

Although raw cotton reported in probate inventories is only a crude indicator of the distribution of cotton among all households, the chart above indicates "cotton woole" is readily available over the period. In certain areas, such as Plymouth and in Essex County (MA), one quarter of all households reported having raw cotton in their households. Clearly, Essex County was a center of cloth-making in Massachusetts, and Salem provided a vital link in the Barbados to Essex County cotton trade. In Suffolk County raw cotton appears in fewer probates, even when the distortion of Boston's transient population is removed. However, the need to promptly process fabric for consumption, as evidenced by Wollcott's yarn and cloth credits with Buffum, may well have made keeping large stocks of raw fiber seem wasteful or unproductive. In Plymouth Colony, the evidence reveals that cotton was a common fiber—nearly as common as wool, hemp or flax. In Connecticut, although the probate data are limited, the existence of raw cotton seems to indicate a similar interest in cotton textiles.

In an account book kept by merchant Peter Berkeley, "cotton woole" was well represented and his accounts are particularly revealing. In his "Third Booke of Accompts," Berkeley recorded the sale of over 180 pounds of cotton to 16 different customers who purchased about 4 pounds each transaction in the period 1680–81. Some of the accounts were settled with cotton stockings produced, presumably, from the original cotton.[22]

A factor that may have influenced the time interval that cotton fiber remained unspun and stored in New England homes and warehouses was the relative ease with which it was turned into yarn. Long before the cotton arrived in New England, the pre-spinning preparation of the fiber began. Picked when the "bolls" began to burst open, Caribbean slaves extracted the long, silky cotton fibers from their seed shell and then from the seeds.[23] The separated cotton fibers were then packed into bales that weighed from about 300 to 400 pounds each. Consequently, the baled "cotton woole" that arrived in New England was ready to be carded and spun into thread without lengthy preparations.

Cotton was prepped for spinning in much the same way as sheep's wool. Just as vegetable fibers were teased out of the raw wool, stray seeds or seed cases were removed before the clean cotton was carded. Unlike wool, there was no grease or dirt to scour out, so the cleaning and carding process was swift. Cotton cards were similar in design to those used for wool except that the spacing between the "combing" nails or wires was more compact due to the finer cotton strands. The small rolls created with the carded cotton would be put aside until they could be spun.[24] The relatively recent arrival of cotton as a textile fiber in England probably meant that English spinners, including English colonials, more than likely used their traditional wool-spinning equipment, a great wheel, for their work rather than a specific wheel type. Cotton required a slightly different spinning technique from that of wool, but not necessarily a specialized spinning wheel.[25] Lacking the scales found on wool fibers and having a relatively short staple length, handspun cotton thread was initially not considered strong enough to be used as a single warp, but it could be plied for strength and used in some instances.[26] Generally, cotton yarn was used as weft on a warp of strong linen threads. This "mixed cloth" was doubtless the first use of cotton both in Old and New England. Despite its growing popularity in the colony, by its very nature cotton only supported and extended the use of the mainstays in English textiles: hemp and flax.

Just as probate inventories contained wool, sheep and cotton, they also included flax fibers from the first days of settlement.

As Chart 8 indicates, inventories reported to the probate courts contained frequent references to flax fibers in household inventories over the period. Most, if not all, of reported fiber was probably dressed and ready to be spun. Although the inventory listers made few distinctions between dressed or unprocessed flax, most of the flax they found was stored in garret rooms, unlikely places for undressed sheaves or unbroken retted flax.

Another way to analyze the flax reported in probate inventories is in average volume per household.

For each sample of New England inventories, a consistent number emerges in Chart 9 of approximately two pounds per average household reporting flax in the first two decades. Again, certain regions within the Bay Colony produced and utilized flax and linen fibers at different rates. For instance, Suffolk County averages increased over the period of study

Chart 8. Number of Probate Inventories Reporting Flax

Year	Bay Colony	Plymouth	Connecticut
1630–49	22/189—12%	5/37—14%	10/46—22%
1650–69	106/1029—11%	38/130—29%	3/16—19%
1670–89	193/1302—15%	n/a	1/18—6%

Chart 9. Average Volume of Flax Fiber Reported in Pounds

Year	Bay Colony	Plymouth	Connecticut
1630–49	239# (2#)	85# (2.3#)	93# (2#)
1650–69	1127# (1.5#)	427# (3.2#)	22# (7.3#)
1670–89	2694# (2#)	n/a	10# (10#)

Chart 10. Number of Probates Reporting Linen Yarns

Year	Bay Colony	Plymouth	Connecticut
1630–49	21/189—11%	5/37—14%	10/46—22%
1650–69	88/1029—9%	29/130—22%	2/16—13%
1670–89	115/1302—9%	n/a	1/18—6%

to exceed Essex County in the last period. The presence of larger quantities of dressed flax in Boston probates indicates that town-dwelling textile producers may have purchased dressed flax from merchants with connections to outlying farms. Moreover, production of finished yarns and fabrics seemed to happen more frequently in Suffolk County. There may well have been a greater demand for linen yarn among lace knitters or frame stocking knitters in the Boston area that inflated Suffolk County's demand for dressed flax.[27]

For the average farmstead, however, two pounds of dressed flax fibers was typical. Two pounds of dressed fiber could be spun into two pounds of yarn with little waste. Two pounds of yarn could become 10 yards of woven cloth.

As Chart 10 demonstrates, linen yarn stocks could be found in approximately 10 percent of all Massachusetts households, with higher numbers in Plymouth and Connecticut. This yarn represents reflects the general nature of linen yarn production. As already observed, linen yarn could be woven into a variety of finished goods. If each household's yarn stocks only equaled the average holding of dressed flax, the annual yield based on those figures alone would mean significant additions to textile stores in the colony. As we have seen, depending on the width of the fabric and the intricacy of the weave, two pounds of linen yarn, spun very fine, could produce ten yards of plain weave linen. Such an amount could be made into four men's shirts or several petticoats and shifts for a woman. Ten yards could also be made into a pair of sheets and pillow beers.[28]

In general, across the sample of probate inventory records, linen yarns were typically present in similar quantities; linen textiles were an important priority for many households. Linen cloth was a source of income as well as a reserve source of family wealth. For Suffolk County (MA), the supply of fabric increased markedly towards the end of the period. Perhaps this increase indicates a greater willingness to engage in textile production because of the valuable nature of cloth; it could also have been a response to a renewed economic opportunity.

Chart 11. Number of Probates Reporting Linen Cloth

Year	Bay Colony	Plymouth	Connecticut
1630–49	22/189—12%	8/37—22%	14/46—30%
1650–69	133/1029—13%	36/130—28%	5/16—31%
1670–89	119/1302—9%	n/a	4/18—22%

Since woven fabric was the most frequent use of linen yarn, most yarn generally passed quickly from the spinners to the weavers. Plain and simple linen needs could be manufactured by the local vernacular weaver while the finer fancier fabrics would be produced by the master weaver. Again, we return to the probates for a rough estimate of provincial linen production.

In Massachusetts Bay, the linen yarns evident in Essex County probates did not translate into a larger number of households with linen cloth when compared to Suffolk County. Rather, a slightly larger number of Suffolk County families seem to have consistently held supplies of linen cloth in store. Whether Essex County transformed its cloth into clothing and household goods at a greater rate or sold its surplus to Suffolk County and beyond is not clear.

In Plymouth and Connecticut, the percentage of probates holding new linen cloth is higher, but the size of the samples may have affected the data. What is clear is that the larger percentage of households with linen yarn did translate into a larger number of probates with new linen cloth.

Whether or not colonists kept the linen cloth they produced or circulated it to other areas, the production of that cloth became an important segment of the provincial economy. Beyond the simple tabulation of pounds of fiber, yarn or yards of cloth, the significance of flaxen and hempen linen to the English colonial household can be measured in the effort devoted to its production.

Just as in the production of wool, all the members of the household participated in the manufacturing process and the finer the fabric, the greater the effort. The shared burden of manufacture was not always "promiscuous." Some chores were seen as female, while others remained mainly a male purview. As a sixteenth-century farm manual indicated, customary practice dominated even the planting of the crop:

> Good flax and good hemp, to have of her own,
> in May a good housewife will see it be sown;
> And afterwards trim it to serve at a need,
> the fimble to spin, and the carl for her seed.[29]

Hemp and flax were traditionally sown and harvested by women in England and Thomas Tusser's verse clarifies the duty of the "good housewife." In his world, men's labor broke the soil and prepared the field for planting, but women sowed and tended the hemp and flax crops. In early April after the men plowed and harrowed and while the soil was still moist, housewives and daughters broadcasted last year's seed harvest by hand. The time-honored method of planting was to sow the seeds "thicke upon the ground." This seeding technique enabled the women to force a tall and thin plant profile by creating a crowded growth environment. Tall and thin flax plants meant that once the fibers were extracted, they would also be long and delicate, the basis for smoothly spun thread and fine quality linen. When English women began to raise flax and hemp in New England, they continued to practice the same tried and true methods.

A persistence of English customs is evident in a number of wills that provided family members with precise instructions concerning flax and hemp production. One such will, that of John Dresser the elder, provides us with a blueprint of how the Dresser family organized and rewarded its laborers. In March of 1671 at the age of 70, John Dresser made his will and provided careful instructions to his heirs. Dividing his property between his wife, two surviving sons and one daughter, Dresser carefully outlined each legacy. To his eldest son, John, he added a small bequest to the "considerable estat" previously bestowed him on the advent of his marriage. A younger son, Samuel, was to receive half of all of the land not already in John's possession, making his share about half of the value of his elder brother's. To Elizabeth, an unmarried daughter, Dresser gave £120, about one-fifth of his estate, to be paid over two years out of the farm's produce, especially its linen goods.

Mary Dresser, the children's mother, received the customary recognition of a good wife: one-third of the produce of the home farm and the right to occupy a portion of the house belonging to her son Samuel. In addition, she received the "moveables" of the household, including a large portion of the household linens and the textile tools. Lastly, to ensure that his widow would be able to continue comfortably "dureing hir natturall Life," Dresser instructed John and Samuel to provide their mother with all the essentials: sufficient firewood, fruit from the orchard, leather "to call for as she seeth neede," and ample Indian and English corn. Further, Dresser's sons were to provide enough prepared land for her to "sowe halfe a peck of flax seed yearly."[30] This field would allow her to continue to produce flax and linen fabrics, undoubtedly with the help of her daughter. As a dutiful child, Elizabeth Dresser would have worked beside her mother to produce the yarns and fabrics; eventually these items provided an important portion of her own inheritance. Samuel also benefitted from the portion of linens left after his mother's and sister's shares. Clearly, John Dresser governed a household where men supported as well as benefitted from the labor of their women.

Some of the extant wills are not as specific as Dresser's, but still suggest the same arrangement. John Balch, for instance, reserved the use of two out of his four improved acres for his widow's use along with the house, houselot and outbuildings. Her tenure was protected as long as she did not remarry, and although Balch did not make the terms as explicit as those of John Dresser did, the duties of children to their parents would dictate that Annis Balch's three sons were bound to make the prepared ground available to her as she desired.[31]

Chapter Three
Textile Skills across Place and Time

> ". . . fill my hands with such convenient skill as may conduce to vertue void of shame . . ."
>
> —worked into Loara Standish's sampler, c. 1640–50[1]

As a Puritan minister, Edward Taylor would have heartily approved of the sentiments Loara Standish worked into her sampler design. He may also have fully understood the multiple layers of meaning her spiritual plea contained. On the one hand, Standish's conventional piety can be read as a prayer meant to protect her from idle, perhaps sinful, foolishness. However, just as Taylor connected the mundane duties of a housewife to the loftier spiritual quest of a Puritan minister, the Standish sampler can also be read as an unaffected plea for more earthly skills. Indeed, as she would know from simple observation, a woman's sewing, knitting, embroidery and spinning skills, were crucial to her future family's success and comfort. Consequently, on both sides of the Atlantic, every seventeenth-century Englishwoman's domestic repertoire included some textile expertise, especially spinning. In the raw, often cold, settlements of New England good cloth was especially important.

Yet, textile skills were not strictly female occupations. Indeed, as one historian observed, a quarter of all adult males who came to New England in this period possessed specific cloth-making skills.[2] Skilled cloth-workers of every sort including flax dressers, weavers and fullers emigrated in significant numbers during the Great Migration period. A notable proportion of New England's population arrived with the essential skills needed to develop a provincial cloth industry.[3]

Despite the productive potential of a skilled populace, historians of colonial New England generally hold that the development of a domestic cloth industry in New England "never proved to be more than a disappointment to its promoters."[4] According to this logic, most colonists presumably left the looms and wheels they paid to transport idle and shifted their efforts to produce marketable farm products. Rum, corn, salted beef and barrel staves would then be exchanged for imported English fabrics. In this interpretation, English imports remained the chief source of fabric in New England settlements. First-generation cloth workers who clung to their art became anachronistic. Logically, given this economic climate, few second-generation colonists could be expected to acquire the skills their parents rejected as irrelevant to their lives; this, in turn, would serve to deepen colonial dependence on imported cloth. Thus, Standish may have learned to embroider her sampler, but not to spin the linen threads or weave the simple linen she used in her work.

Yet, evidence from the period suggests that rather than abandon their textile work colonists consistently valued these skills and required their children to learn them. Edward Johnson, an avid chronicler of New England's progress, observed in 1654 that the inhabitants of Rowley, Massachusetts, "caused their little ones to be diligent" in the acquisition of cloth-making skills from their parents for the betterment of the community.[5] Rather than being irrelevant, textile skills served to augment the prosperity of the next generation. Furthermore, the instruction of new textile workers welded household members together, ensured proper order within the household and transferred the key elements of collective and cooperative family labor to the next generation.

Parents began the process of handing on their expertise with the ritualistic yet informal training of very young children. As toddlers, they learned first by observation. Then, as their knowledge, dexterity and strength increased, they were given increasingly complex chores, which passed from father to son, mother to daughter along well-established lines. By the age of five or six, boys accompanied their fathers to workshops and fields; girls learned their future work from their mothers in theirs homes and farmyards. As Plymouth Colony historian John Demos wrote:

> The family was a "vocational institute." . . . [the active transmission of skills] clearly served to prepare its young for effective, independent performance in the larger economic system. For the majority of persons . . . the process was instinctive and almost unconscious.[6]

The "instinctive" and "almost unconscious" nature of children's training has left little in the way of extant documentation. Rather, parental education of children can only be inferred from a scant selection of sources. In his study of male farm labor in seventeenth-century Essex County,

Massachusetts, Daniel Vickers found that although young boys routinely worked alongside their fathers and grandfathers on the land, their presence was mainly implied rather than clearly described. Thus, indirect references locate young boys in the "misty backdrop" of rural farm scenes and the details of their training remain obscure.[7] The training of girls is likewise difficult to document.

One type of record that provides insight into children's "vocational" training is the guardianship petition. These documents were sometimes generated when death or remarriage disrupted the "natural" cycle of parental training. Filed in probate courts, they became legally binding contracts meant to protect the property of the children involved as well as to spell out guardians' responsibilities. In the process, the petitions described the duties of parents towards their children indirectly by laying out the colony's expectations of guardians and foster parents. Formalistic documents framed in legal terms, they carried a clear message: children needed proper training to take up the roles they were expected to play as adults. For girls, this meant sound instruction in domestic arts, with an emphasis on female textile skills. Such was the case concerning the Sharpe children.

In 1656, Peter Aspinwall became the court-appointed guardian of Mary and Abigail, orphaned children of Robert Sharpe. Remarried and worried that her new husband would dissipate her children's property, Abigail Sharpe Clapp requested that Aspinwall, a relative by marriage, take over administration of their affairs. Adopting a "needful and speedy course" to protect the children's welfare, Aspinwall assumed custody of the two girls. In exchange for his efforts and expenditure, Aspinwall requested the court allow him to lease out the house, land and livestock left to the children by their father. He further agreed to use the profits garnered from the farm to support the children while preserving their future security in the form of land and goods. Protection of their property was not the only obligation he assumed towards the children, however. In the official petition, Aspinwall guaranteed he would "learn" the girls to "read, to knit, to spin and such housewifery, and keep them, either to the day of their marriage or until age eighteen."[8]

The court agreed readily to the particulars and the spirit of the petition. First, the two children would be provided suitable care in a reputable home at the expense of their father's estate and would not become a drain on the town's resources. Since Robert Sharpe was deceased and their mother seemingly incapable of providing for the children, this was the next best solution. Second, Aspinwall's "better" socio-economic position, his unimpeachable reputation as a church member, and his elected office in the town ensured that the Sharpe children would live in a scrupulously "ordered" household. Finally, Aspinwall guaranteed that the Sharpe children would be properly trained and educated to take their place in the community as responsible and productive adults.[9]

Aspinwall's commitment carried complex obligations that went far beyond simple nurture and discipline. However, the shifting of responsibility from Sharpe to Aspinwall did not fundamentally change the contours of parental obligation, it merely transferred them. As the petition made clear, textile production figured prominently as skills too important to be lumped in with other "such housewifery." Aspinwall's agreement explicitly outlined duties that most families implicitly accepted; the petition also reflected the expectations of the colony towards their children's training. In a few cases this pattern of explicit responsibility can be traced in specific families.

As an adult, Mary Sharpe found herself repeating her mother's story when she became widowed in 1689. When her husband, Nathaniel Tilden, died, he left her with a partially-grown family consisting of several adult children and two still at home. In his will, Tilden left instructions for their eldest son to take responsibility for the children's material welfare, but left Mary Sharpe Tilden to oversee the "education and Disposeing of them." Perhaps because she did not remarry right away, Tilden did not choose to relinquish the care and education of her children. Unlike her mother, she had the opportunity to pass her skills on directly.[10]

Another source documenting textile skill transmission is the indenture contract; especially those made for indigent female children. Mary Killam, a child "set out" to the Parsons family by the Hampshire County Court (MA), is a case in point. Although the wording of the document deciding her fate corresponded closely to the guardianship papers of Mary and Abigail Sharpe, the Hampshire indenture agreement bound Killam to the service of Samuel Parsons until she was 18. As an unpaid servant, Killam was expected to work hard at whatever Parsons or his wife directed and to expect just punishment if she did not comply. In exchange, Parsons agreed to teach her "to read English, sewing, spinning, and knitting."

What is striking about this indenture is the congruity of domestic skills expected of Mary Killam compared to the Sharpe sisters. Taken from a family where frequent removals implied an unstable and impoverished life, Mary Killam still needed this expertise whether she married or spent her life as a servant. Just as in the Sharpe document, female textile skills figured prominently, underscoring their importance to New Englanders yet again.[11]

Girls' domestic textile instruction occurred in a variety of settings. Most started training under their mother's supervision, but they may have perfected their skills in the company of other women. In the case of Betsey and Abigail Sharpe, their mother surely began the process since they were five and seven when they moved to the Aspinwall household; undoubtedly the girls underwent expanded instruction with their foster mother.

As was the case for all crafts, skills necessary to cloth manufacture accumulated gradually. As a child progressed in age, so would the difficulty of her activity. The simplest tasks generally were associated with the medial processing of wool, flax and cotton fibers after harvest, but before spinning and weaving. Picking and carding wool, for instance, required only a limited degree of manual dexterity, no skill, and only minimal supervision. A busy housewife with young daughters like the Sharpe girls could set them to the task of carding the family's wool and then turn to younger infants, dairy chores or sundry other household work with only cursory attention to the girls' carding. The same was true for the carding of raw cotton.

Hackling broken flax, another intermediate chore, required more expertise and concentration. This process was a more precise chore. As we have seen, the hackler sorted fibers in a progressive combing process. The flax passed through a series of ever-finer combs, which separated the coarse from the fine fibers. The different quality flax fibers served various uses from candlewicks to fine linen thread. Here, more careful and persistent supervision was required or an entire year's flax crop could be spoiled. An unskilled child put to the task of hackling her mother's or mistress' flax crop could seriously damage the plant fibers and potentially ruin the linen thread or separate the chaff so badly that the fibers were only useful as candle wicks.

Eventually, young women took up spinning and learned to produce yarn. A universal female skill, spinning benefited households of every economic level and at every stage of life. Young housewives with infant children were especially likely to embrace spinning as a sidebar handicraft in a youthful household. As historian Laurel Ulrich has observed:

> The Graftons [a couple who lived in Salem in the last half of the 17th century] had neither [sheep nor a loom in the shed]. Children—not sheep—put wheels in Hannah [Grafton]'s house. The mechanical nature of spinning made it a perfect occupation for women whose attention was engrossed by young children.[12]

For mothers whose daughters were old enough to begin spinning, instruction provided an opportunity to teach the female virtues of perseverance, patience and humility as well as an important skill. Part of the constellation of a good housewife's domestic arts, spinning could also serve to extend a young woman's bride wealth by allowing her to earn money or accumulate textile items of her own. Consider, for instance, Reverend Barnard of Andover and his hired girls.

Over a number of seasons in the 1690s, Barnard hired young women who came into his home to spin and knit. In just one month, November of 1693, he paid wages to eight different women for their part in the production of approximately 20 pounds of finished yarn.[13] Coming to work on the four spinning wheels found in his home, these young women probably viewed their opportunity to "help" at the Barnard home as a respectable option open to unmarried females and a source of important income for their families.

The yarn produced by Barnard's hired girls was worsted wool harvested from a leased flock. Barnard's final "reckoning" with his landlord occurred in the fall of 1692, so the wool harvested the next spring was entirely his own. The spinners worked on the washed, picked and carded wool that probably amounted to his entire wool clip, about 35 to 40 pounds of prepared wool. At two shillings per pound, Barnard offered the standard wage for the period, although his account book only recorded the wage values, not how the girls were paid. However Barnard compensated the young women, his use of the neighborhood skills to turn his raw wool into finished yarn was part of a cycle of related activities that drove the engine of the local economy. Without the transmission of textile skills from one generation to the next, Barnard, a second-generation planter, could not have benefitted from a neighborhood network of laboring girls.

Barnard was by no means an exception. Householders regularly profited from the textile labors of their wives and daughters. Such was the case of Renold Foster, a respected freeman of Ipswich, Massachusetts. The owner of a "better" estate valued at over seven hundred pounds, Foster died in June 1681. Rich in textiles of all types, Foster's estate included at least four complete sets of bedding with linen sheets, embroidered coverlets, bed curtains and wool blankets. In addition, there were linen tablecloths ("boardcloths"), towels and napkins and new linen yardage. Fully 30 percent of the value of Foster's "movable" estate was in textiles. While undoubtedly some of these were imported, it is also clear that locally-produced cloth contributed in important ways to the value of Foster's estate.

Quite likely, Sarah and Mary Foster spent many hours under their mother's eye as they processed wool harvested from their father's flock into yarn that later became broadcloth, knitted stockings or blankets. Although the inventory does not specifically include spinning wheels, the presence of over ten pounds of wool yarn and 16 pounds of raw wool indicates some access to equipment, perhaps at a neighbor's home.

Linens were also produced locally, employing at least some of the household's female labor. Again, the absence of equipment would seem to make linen production less likely; yet Foster specifically pointed out his wife and daughters' involvement. In his will, he gave all the "linnen and woollen yarne, *that she hath made* [my emphasis]" to his wife.

In more than one instance, Foster conceded that his textile wealth had mainly been "provided into the house" by his wife and daughters. To acknowledge each of his daughters' labors, Foster divided a substantial portion of the sheets, blankets and table linen between them as part of their share of his estate. In this case, the linens accounted for £10 of each daughter's inheritance.

To his wife, Foster left a variety of linens and bedclothes that allowed her a comfortable life and, in addition, he protected her future productivity. In final instructions via his will, Foster charged his executors, sons Joseph and Abraham, to provide their mother with wool from his flock and to prepare adequate land for her flax crop. Moreover, he attempted to ensure that an aging Sarah, lacking unmarried daughters would have extra "help" in her textile labors.

The only set of linens willed outside the immediate family was a "bed bolster, pillow and paire of sheets of my now wives makeing." This, he reserved for his granddaughter, Hannah Story. Although Hannah was not his only grandchild, nor even his only female grandchild, Foster singled her out precisely for the same reasons he handed the manufactured textiles over to his daughters: Hannah Story lived and worked in her grandparents' home. This is evident in the stipulation made by Foster that she would be entitled to her legacy only if she remained in her grandmother's home to help "as she hath done to us hitherto." Undoubtedly Story "helped" her grandmother with textile tasks that did not stop when the Foster children were grown and gone to families of their own. Hence, in the careful distribution of his estate, Foster asserted the important contribution of the women in his household as well as the value of his household's textiles.[14]

Most women never saw their labors directly acknowledged. For instance, John Gould, a Topsfield, Massachusetts, weaver and sheep owner, recorded credit in his account book for more than ten pounds of spun yarn from "Uncle Andrew." Since men did not spin, it seems likely that it was the women of Andrew Gould's household who provided the skills and labor for credit on the Gould household account. On another page, a similar entry indicated that "Brother Thomas" was credited for spinning twelve and a half pounds of combed flax.[15] In the case of hired women, their labor was even more obscure.

Just as Mary Killam anonymously contributed to the wealth of the Parsons family as a poor young servant, so did many young women whose work went largely unrecorded. Only a few criminal and civil court records reveal tiny glimpses of these female workers. At various times, young women showed up in court proceedings as witnesses, defendants and plaintiffs; in their testimony their labors became a matter of record.

Mary Walcott, a young Salem, Massachusetts, woman, sat "composed and knitting" while she claimed to be tormented by one of the accused witches, Goody Cloyse.[16] At the time of her testimony, Mary knitted yarn under the supervision of the wife of her employer, Thomas Putnam. Yet, Mary could very well have learned to knit and to spin in her own home, since yarn and knitted stockings were among the products frequently used to settle her father's accounts with Phillip English, another Salem merchant.[17]

Mary Warren, a servant in the house of John Proctor, was among the initial group of "afflicted" girls who accused neighborhood men and women of witchcraft in early 1692. Her angry employer claimed in court that her "possession" was really malicious mischief since as long as he kept her "close to her wheel," Warren did not have time to think of witchcraft or have "fitts."[18] Apparently Proctor was forced to demand textile labors from his hired girl. When he was not around to police her behavior, she avoided such work altogether. Ironically, Proctor became the victim of her willful behavior when she accused him of being a witch; subsequently found guilty, he was the first man to be executed in the 1692 incident.[19]

While one woman's spinning kept her from "possession," another woman's was proof of enchantment. Rebecca Stearns was unable to make her spinning wheel work properly and, at first, thought it was "out of kilter." Both she and her husband, Charles Stearns, attempted to put it right, but with little success. They began to suspect external causes. At one moment the wheel worked fine, while the next Rebecca Stearns "could make no work of it." Soon, she became convinced her wheel was enchanted by her neighbor, Winifred Holman. In the face of Stearns' need to "spin for the necesity of her family," she demanded that Holman be charged and convicted of witchcraft.[20]

In still another case of suspected witchcraft, William Browne repeatedly harassed a young married neighbor, Goody Prince. After her child was stillborn, Prince claimed that Browne caused the death of her child with a curse. The neighborhood divided over the case with much testimony on both sides. Abigail Seargeant, a woman who gave evidence in defense of Browne, maintained that Prince brought the stillbirth upon herself by engaging in labors too difficult for her stage of pregnancy, including spinning for long hours.[21] Browne was never formally charged and the complaint lodged by Margaret Prince was eventually dismissed, but Seargeant's observation reminds us of the daily toil faced by young housewives. Prince's prodigious spinning represented only a small portion of her workload and may even have been in anticipation of the new baby and an expansion of textile needs in the Prince household.

Although girls were never formally apprenticed to learn textile skills, guardianship petitions, indenture contracts and court transcripts clearly indicate that New England homes customarily engaged in female textile instruction. As a result, most New England women possessed the basic skills to produce yarn, the primary element of fabric. Some of that yarn was fashioned into knitted stockings, shawls, mittens and mufflers, but woven fabric was also necessary. In this way, weavers were as essential to New England's textile industry as spinners.

Since the bulk of the "great migration" immigrants hailed from the cloth-making regions of England, it is no great surprise that weavers comprised more than sixteen percent of the many skilled artisans who decided to emigrate.[22] These skilled immigrant craftsmen brought the expertise and equipment needed to produce finished cloth. Yet along with the tools of their trade, they also needed farm equipment and animals. Conditions of settlement made it necessary to engage in simple agriculture to guarantee food supplies each year. Thus, many weavers and cloth finishers continued to practice their craft in Massachusetts even as they cleared farmlands and developed adequate food supplies.

A crude census of occupations provides some evidence for the persistence of New England fancy weavers in their trade. In a sample of 464 Massachusetts Bay inventories, 40 men (approximately 13%) reported their occupation as "weaver."[23] In Essex County (MA), the percentage of first generation weavers corresponds with the percentage of self-identified weavers who originally emigrated. A sample of 164 Plymouth Colony inventories, reveal the presence of at least five well-appointed weavers' shops in the years between 1633–1669.[24] In nearby Connecticut, the probate records are less revealing, but a sample of 80 probate inventories revealed the estates of 4 weavers, 3 who lived in Hartford and one in Farmington.[25] In addition, there were a number of inventories taken of individuals who lived outside of Hartford and Farmington that contained references to yarn "out at the weavers." Rhode Island historian Carl Bridenbaugh identified 9 weavers from among the 93 artisans enumerated between 1638–1690.[26] Clearly, many of the first-generation craftsmen were able to resume weaving at some point in their lives.

Certainly the area a particular craftsman chose for settlement distinctly influenced how well he was able to continue his craft. It is difficult to know whether individuals realized this as they assembled their new towns or simply took their chances. Only in the case of the people of Rowley, Massachusetts, do we know that textile production was uppermost in their minds as they selected their settlement site and organized their new town. Yet, at least some weavers knew they would continue in their craft, because towns very often recruited weavers and their families to settle in exchange for land.

In 1656, the inland town of Chelmsford, Massachusetts, admitted William Howe as a free inhabitant and granted him 12 acres of meadow and 12 acres of upland meadow "provided he set up his trade of weaving and perform[ed] the towne's work."[27] In Ipswich, Massachusetts, the town not only granted land, but also saw to the practical matters of buildings as well. In 1671, the town gave James Sawyer, one of at least three resident weavers, the right to fell enough trees from the common to build a little "shope" for his looms next to his home.[28] Two other seventeenth-century Ipswich weavers, Thomas Lull and Nathaniel Fuller, were regularly granted the right to fell pine trees from the town's common in amounts that equaled the claims of "ancient" commoners.[29] Clearly, the weaving trade allowed them privileges meant for valuable citizens.

Access to land and buildings did not create a class of wealthy weavers in New England, however. For the most part weaving remained an occupation for a middling tradesman. A sampling of the probates of identified weavers indicates that the median probate value was fewer than £200; only a few boasted inventories above £200 and none held estates valued over £500.[30] The range of actual living standards among weaving households can be seen in the difference between three representative households from the period.

Thomas Payne, a first generation emigrant, brought his skills and equipment with him when he came to New England in 1638 aboard the *Mary Anne*. Apprenticed in Suffolk, England, Payne settled in Salem and prospered. In his will, dated 1638, he left a house and two-acre houselot with gardens in Salem and more in planting land and meadow outside the village. Additional investments in shipping and a gristmill provided the basis for his sons' legacies, which were to be paid out of the sale proceeds. To his eldest son he also gave his weaving equipment that consisted of several looms and assorted "appurtenances" belonging thereto.

The existence of his "well-appointed" shop demonstrates that Payne was a professional weaver, although he probably managed a small farm to provide his home with foodstuffs as well. The success of Payne's strategy is evident in the breadth of his estate, including property and moveable goods aplenty. His craft evidently continued to serve him well, even after his move to New England. The most telling evidence of the lasting worth of Payne's vocation was son Thomas's adoption of his father's trade.[31]

A second weaver's estate provides us with a more detailed inventory. Before his death in 1673, Francis Plummer of Newbury managed a weaver's shop as well as a substantial farm. Since all we have is the list of his property and goods, there is no way to know how and when he accumulated the farmland and which came first, the trade or his property. It seems likely, though, that he was a weaver first. Plummer may have been a first-generation arrival with skills or he may have arrived apprenticed to another master weaver. His property was most likely accumulated after reaching adulthood and, since Plummer had at least two grown sons and perhaps several step-sons as well, he could have developed the farm as they matured. It is clear from his inventory that Plummer maintained a weaving shop attached to his home where his looms and equipment were set up. This would seem to indicate that although he probably supervised the operation of his land and farm, he was also a full-time weaver and perhaps even supervised an apprentice.

The general textile wealth of the household also implies Plummer's skill. Sheets, tablecloths, coverlets and clothing amounted to over £40 and accounted for fully 10 percent of the total inventory's value. Moreover, Plummer's wife and daughters may have helped in the shop as they certainly had access to the spinning equipment and raw materials listed in the inventory.[32]

The third set of documents, an inventory and proofs of John Kingsbery of Rowley, gives us an example of a young and relatively poor weaving household.[33] Kingsbery died suddenly in the winter of 1670 leaving his wife and two small children with a small estate valued at only £66. Although he owned 40 acres of "wilderness" land, Kingsbery lived in a small house built on one acre in Rowley village that housed his family and his weaving shop. With only a few livestock and rights to one acre of common pasture, he obviously made his living as a weaver. Indeed the most valuable grouping of moveable goods in the inventory was his loom, collection of reeds and other weaving "tackle," totaling over £4.

Yet, this may have been an upwardly mobile household rather than a stagnantly poor one. With barrels of salted meat and dried corn put by as well as a small but adequate assortment of cooking utensils, the Kingsberys were obviously able to feed themselves quite well. The "bead and clothes" valued at 10 percent of the total inventory indicate that at least some of the comforts of a middling household existed in the Kingsbery home. Moreover, the purchase of "wilderness" land for his children's future indicated Kingsbery's ability to increase his assets from profits earned with his craft.

Still more significant is the second-generation status of John Kingsbery. He clearly did not emigrate with his skills; instead he apprenticed and trained in New England. Kingsbery chose to become a weaver and must have perceived it as a viable opportunity for success, not a moribund craft. Indeed, his untimely death, not his choice of occupation, seems to have been the greatest blow to his family's prosperity.

The experiences of Payne, Plummer and Kingsbery suggest that first-generation emigrants who practiced their trade did not simply weave, but also created the next generation of weavers. Second- and third-generation craftsmen enhanced the production of established workshops and became replacements when their masters retired. Moreover, in the shops of such men, weaving skills could be transmitted in either of two ways: a formal apprenticeship contract or casual transmission among family members.

In formal apprenticeships, boys were generally "put out" to live in the home of a master weaver. The young apprentice went to his master in much the same way that Mary Killam went to the Parsons home, "living in" with the master craftsman's household for the duration of the agreement. As in Killam's court-imposed indenture, the apprenticeship contract provided for specific obligations on both sides. For the young apprentice, the contract outlined the length of training period and his expected "graduation" to the next stage of his occupation. For his part, the master craftsman agreed to teach the "mysteries" of his craft from winding quills to warping a loom to the making of "sleyes." Very often the master agreed as part of his obligations to provide the successful young journeyman weaver with his own loom at the end of his contract. In exchange, the apprentice weaver agreed to work diligently for his master for a prescribed period of time, faithfully endeavor to learn his appointed trade and respect his master's authority as he would his father's. The successful master craftsman could have more than one apprentice at one time and employed a journeyman weaver, giving him greater productive capacity than he had on his own. For a master who could not afford the expense of an apprentice, there were other alternatives.

Very often, members of a weaver's family learned the skills of the trade without formalized training. Frequently the entire household, including the women, would have their turn at winding quills, warping the loom or weaving a "web of cloth."[34] Given the seasonal nature of the production and processing of textile fibers, certain times of the year likely brought heavier demands and forced all available hands into the work. Even more possible, the different cloth requirements from simple tabby weaves to more intricate designs caused many weavers to set adolescent children or wives unencumbered by infants at the looms for the simpler work while they labored over the more elaborate compositions. Interested children, especially a son like that of Thomas Payne, could become their father's apprentices without formal contract and be trained to inherit the father's business as well.

One such household was that of Thomas Chittenden of Scituate. A weaver with a considerable array of "tooles," he judiciously divided the textile tools between his two sons, Isaac and Henry:

> Item: I give unto my son Isacke one loome to my son henery one loome; and my mind and will is that hee that posesseth the great loome shall pay ten shillings to him that hath the lesser or shorter loome. Item: I give and bequeath unto my son henery all the slayes and implements of the shop and my will is that my sonne henery pay to his brother Isacke thirty shillings in Consideration thereof; and alow Isacke to make use of the slayes soe longe as they Conveniently live together as hitherto he hath had: provided That Isacke alow his brother henery to make use of his slayes as hitherto he hath Done.[35]

Clearly both Henry and Isaac Chittenden learned their weaving from their father, Thomas. In his will, Thomas tried to apportion enough of the equipment (or allow for the purchase of replacement equipment) for each to have his own start. It is clear that Thomas hoped his sons would continue to ply their trade together, but it is also evident that he intended that neither of them would be left without the means to continue if they could no longer work together.

The Lawes family of Salem engaged in both kinds of skill transmission. Born in or around 1586, Francis Lawes left home and apprenticed as a weaver in the English manufacturing center of Norwich. A bustling community of traders and artisans as well as a well-known textile-producing center, Norwich provided Lawes with the opportunity to set up his own shop and, presumably, to take in apprentices of his own. By 1637, Lawes, a middle-aged master craftsman and freeman of Norwich, had at least one apprentice, Samuel Lincoln, in his shop. In that same year, Lawes sailed aboard *The Rose* to New England taking his wife, daughter, a woman servant and his apprentice, Lincoln. Lawes must have been a fairly successful weaver since he was able to finance the passage of his family of three plus two retainers. Upon arrival, Lawes still had enough cash to purchase a houselot in Salem.[36]

In Massachusetts Bay, Lawes continued weaving full-time and informally trained at least two more people, his daughter, Mary, and her son, John Neale. Lawes hoped John Neale would carry on in the family trade and so left all his "weaueing Tackling as Loomes, slease, harnes & what euer elce belongs unto" to him. From the inventory of John Neale, Jr.'s estate in 1679, it seems clear that Neale did not pursue his grandfather's craft. Instead, Neale must have honored the clause in his grandfather's will that if he did not "make use of it himself," the loome and all its attendant parts would revert to Lawes' daughter, Mary, for her "use and dispose."[37]

Mary Neale did use her father's loom and prodigiously. When her husband died in 1672, his inventory included a long list of table and bedlinens as well as 12 yards of "hoame-made" cloth. While Mary's work may not have been professional in the sense she was never a formal apprentice and could not aspire to "master weaver" as John Neale might have done, her textile work was still important. The handmaiden to the professional weaver, the home vernacular weaver or "cottage weaver" worked on simple fabrics—often with a counter-balanced loom limited to two basic weave structures: plain (tabby) weave and balanced twill. As a "cottage weaver" Mary Lawes Neale's "hoame-made" cloth was an important asset to the household as she would have, at the least, woven sheets, towels, blanketing and other simple tabby or twill fabrics. Indeed, her own inventory made nine years later, reveals an additional harvest of linens and woolens worth about £25. Moreover, Mary's skill became the next generation's legacy when she passed on her loom, not to her son John, but to her step-son, Samuel Mansfield.

Shortly after the death of her first husband, John Neale, Sr., Mary Lawes Neale remarried. Her second husband was Andrew Mansfield, a widower with children from his first marriage. One of his adolescent children, Samuel, must have become interested in weaving and may even have trained as an apprentice somewhere in the neighborhood. When he married in 1676 and presumably set up in his own household, his step-mother passed Francis Lawes' loom on to him.[38] When Samuel Mansfield died in a smallpox epidemic in 1679, he left his loom and all of its tackling surrounded by the appurtenances of an active weaver's shop.[39] So, despite the Neale family disinterest, Mary Lawes still found an heir to her father's legacy.

Unlike the Lawes, the Stickney family did not come to New England with an obvious tradition of weaving. Instead, faced with the need to settle a large brood of nine children, William Stickney apprenticed one of his younger sons, Amos, to a local weaver, possibly James Howe. Providing the apprenticeship and the wherewithal to set up, William believed himself discharged of his parental duty when he "procured [Amos] a trade and given him some part of estat toward his settleing" and added a token of "but five pounds more," in his will.[40]

Amos Stickney doubtless consented to the plan or perhaps even solicited his father's help in obtaining the apprenticeship. Most apprenticeships were arranged by parents, but frequently after a child's interest has been expressed. Further, cooperation on the part of the apprentice was necessary in the completion of a successful contract. However, the best evidence for Amos Stickney's enthusiasm was his probate inventory. Replete with yarn supplies, new cloth and a "loame with all tackling for weaving," the inventory of his weaving shop suggests customary activity rather than neglect.[41]

In a similar situation, George Abbott apprenticed one of his 11 children, a younger son named Obed, to be a weaver. Training in Salem, Abbott chose to stay on there after his apprenticeship was over. Perhaps the bustling port town was the right choice since he was able to accumulate enough savings to purchase a house and 63 acres of land in Billerica by 1725.[42]

Not all apprenticeships passed smoothly. In February of 1664, Joseph Pike agreed to teach Samuel Hadley the "trade of a weaver." In the contract written up by Pike and George Hadley, Samuel's father, Pike furthermore agreed to provide his apprentice with a "good loom with the tackling and a good shuttle fit to set to work with."[43] For the next five years, Hadley lived in Pike's Newbury home learning his craft and, according to Hadley, weaving "all that was wove in the house" because "his mastar Could not abide to weave."[44] Towards the end of his indenture, Hadley claimed that he could weave at least ten yards of cloth a day and could warp a loom as proficiently as his employer.

As he reached the end of his apprenticeship to Pike, Hadley made plans to begin his "journeyman" work. At the invitation of John Knight, Hadley agreed to set up his loom at Knight's home and weave him a "web of Cloth." Returning to Pike's for his equipment, he apparently found Pike unwilling to live up to his end of the bargain and provide Hadley with a "good loom."

Since the original agreement concerned Joseph Pike and Samuel's father, George Hadley, Samuel turned to his father for help. Not being a weaver himself, the elder Hadley enlisted the help of a Rowley weaver, John Howe. Howe and Hadley visited with Pike attempting to settle the dispute, but found him intractable. First, Pike claimed Hadley had not fulfilled the terms of the indenture. Pronouncing that Samuel was incorrigible, Pike attempted to convince the elder Hadley and Howe that his best teaching efforts went unrewarded. When two men pressed Pike further on the issue of Samuel's behavior, Pike admitted Hadley had not truly violated his contract obligations. Then, when prodded by Howe and Hadley to fulfill his part of the covenant, Pike tried to pass off an old loom "standing in a hovel which seem[ed] to be rotten and ready to fall to pieces."

Leaving Pike's home dissatisfied, the elder Hadley filed suit at the Ipswich Quarterly Court. Under the examination by the magistrates, the testimony ranged from the depositions of witnesses to the presentation of the original apprenticeship document. Finally, in the face of the evidence presented, the judges decided in favor of Samuel Hadley. Following their decision, the court ordered Pike to provide a "good loom with all things fitting for it" within the month.

The protracted testimony demonstrated more than Pike's parsimonious nature. Apparently, although he "could not abide to weave," Pike did not give up his craft. This suggests that occupations were not so easily discarded upon arrival in New England. Furthermore, although Pike owned some land and farmed it, he continued to get his living primarily by weaving. Pike's agreement to train Samuel Hadley may have freed him to do more of his farm work or may also have been the result of neighborhood pressure to guarantee continued service as in the case of the Chelmsford weaver, William Howe.[45] Despite his own shortcomings, Pike helped to expand the pool of native-born craftsmen manufacturing domestic cloth.

As apprentices became journeymen, they needed to establish economic relationships that allowed them to pursue their craft. Often apprentices simply stayed with their master until they were able to set up in their own right. However, journeymen weavers also moved about New England in search of work and perhaps to establish a connection in a new town. Certainly Samuel Hadley attempted to set up and ply his trade, probably as a journeyman, when he ran into his difficulties with Mr. Pike.

The account book of Christopher Leffingwell, a Hartford area weaver, records an agreement between himself and a journeyman weaver, John Birchard.

> February 14, 1698/9, Then agreed with John Birchard for a years' work
> he to weave eight yards per day of such cloth as is 5d p yard weaving
> and proportionately of other work constantly except publick days and
> he is to have for his wages a part of the weaving work to himself to the
> value of fifteen pounds.[46]

Presumably, Leffingwell provided Birchard with more than just a place to work. Over the year or more that he spent in Leffingwell's shop, Birchard could have benefitted from the superior knowledge and skill of his master, learned new weaving patterns and gained valuable experience.

Parental instruction, apprenticeships and indentures all yielded the same result. Second- and third-generation colonists learned the skills necessary to produce domestic cloth and practiced them. The result was an extensive provincial cloth industry that crossed gender lines and involved in one way or another almost every household in New England. To some colonists the absence of a large export industry in textiles may have been a disappointment. Certainly, the textile producers of New England worked primarily to fulfill local needs. Yet, those needs were extensive and demanded an enormous effort from a highly integrated workforce. The success of the industry was obvious to the largest proportion of settlers. To them, the 10 to 20 percent of increased personal wealth furnished by domestic manufactured cloth, not to mention the additional comfort, was sufficient to the day. Just as important, New England's provincial cloth manufacture spared frugal colonists from squandering their hard-earned coin on simple needs they could produce themselves.

Chapter Four

The Organization of Production

"these people being very industrious every way . . . set upon the making of cloth . . . , and caused their little-ones to be dilligent.
—Captain Edward Johnson, 1651[1]

Social historians who have studied early New England have variously described the provincial economy as a matter of household labor, family labor and even gender specific labor. Certainly individual households were settings within which the labor of textile production took place. Yet the organizational structure of textile work was not necessarily an embodiment of the "little commonwealth" imagined by some historians. The image of a colonial household as an "absolutely central agency of economic production and exchange [where] . . . [e]ach household was more or less self-sufficient; and its various members were inextricably united in the work of providing for their material wants . . ." has been particularly enduring, but this view contradicts the larger corporate effort necessary for survival in New England.[2] Certainly family members worked together to a degree under the direction of the patriarch to provide for the needs of the household. However, this model of a self-contained and self-directed economic unit does not fit with the larger pattern of cloth-making. The very nature of England's and New England's textile-manufacturing networks meant that individuals were brought into the web of production at different points and under varying degrees of supervision. In this way, textile production demanded that colonial households be scenes of extensive as well as intensive human relations that routinely stretched into the homes of their neighbors. The basic fact of life in seventeenth-century New England was that no single household produced cloth by itself.

No less misleading is the gender-segregated world so gracefully teased from the pages of Martha Ballard's diary. Laurel Ulrich's vision of women circulating among neighborhood homes to work in female-segregated groups conjures a New England where men and women's work worlds remain largely gender exclusive.

> [Female] community life [had as its base] a gender division of labor that gave them responsibility for particular tasks, products, and forms of trade. . . . Men broke flax, sheared sheep, and performed other supportive services, but women had primary responsibility for the production of cloth.[3]

For historians who have rightly sought to replace women in the historical landscape, this view is persuasive. Women did indeed engage in sex-specific tasks and work in sex-segregated groups at times. Yet, this view precludes the close male/female collaboration in sheep raising, flax agriculture and the outright sharing of textile processing chores. This is not to argue that women's active role in colonial public society, especially as textile producers, is less. Rather, that men and women often worked closely together in order to accomplish the larger goal. Without such "promiscuous" activities, New Englanders simply could not produce enough domestic cloth for their needs. Dividing textile chores sharply along gender lines diminishes the breadth of colonial cloth making.

More than the work of any single gender or household, domestic cloth production was visible in nearly every part of New England's social landscape. Elements of textile work could be found on farms where shepherds cared for their flocks and in gardens where women harvested their flax and hemp. Barns and lofts were sites where men and women began the first steps of fiber processing. In the garrets and great rooms of individual homes, families stored distaffs crowned with fine blond flax strands and baskets filled with fluffy cotton and wool rolls until they could be spun into yarn. Housewives and their daughters turned and treadled their spinning wheels in their sunny dooryards or in front of a warm hearth of an evening. In shops and garret rooms professional and vernacular weavers worked huck-a-buck and diaper designs into the cloth stretched on their looms surrounded by wives and children winding quills and preparing new warps. Along the banks of New England's rivers mill wheels chattered and turned the machinery inside the braking and fulling mills of the cloth dressers. Indeed, the manufacturing of textiles wove a richly intricate tapestry drawing individuals, neighborhoods, communities and even regions into its web.

As a provincial industry and part of New England's larger economy, textile production concerned more than just the shepherd, housewife or clothier; it was also the business of colonial leaders. In Massachusetts, the provincial government recognized the importance of provincial textiles and their political actions directed the overall pattern of production. Within a decade of the arrival of the Winthrop fleet, the Court began to concentrate on development of the industry.

> The Court taking into serious consideration the absolute necessity for the raising of the manufacture of linen cloth, etc. doth declare that it is the intent of this Court that there shall be an order setled about it, and therefore doth require the magistrats and deputies of the several towns to acquaint the townesmen therewith and to make inquiry . . . , what men and women are skillful in the braking, spinning, weaving; what means for the providing of wheeles; and to consider with those skillful in that manufacture, and what course may be taken for teaching boys and girls in all townes the spinning of the yarn; and to return to the next Court their several and joynt advise about this thing.[4]

In effect, the magistrates attempted to produce a survey of the potential for textile manufacturing that could then inform their management at the provincial level. The study must have revealed an obvious potential for cloth making since the next announcement offered production incentives.

In October of the same year, the Court instituted a bounty of three pence for every shilling's worth of fabric produced. Several stipulations dictated how bonus fabric would be defined. "[T]he cloth must be made within the jurisdiction and the yarne heare spun alsoe, and of such materials as shall be also raised within the same, or else of cotton."[5]

These incentive payments continued to be paid for a little more than a year until the Court, under pressure from an economic recession, repealed the order. Nevertheless, a considerable number of men were able to claim sizable bounties before the court revoked its obligation. Among these, John Whitredge, an Ipswich man, collected payment for the manufacture of over 80 yards of fabric produced in 1641.[6]

Over the next decade, the Court authorized multiple ordinances designed to encourage development of domestic textile resources as well as to seek out and promote necessary skills. While some historians have dismissed these as futile attempts to entice reluctant colonists into cloth manufacture, the cumulative effects of these various pieces of legislation would seem to indicate otherwise.

For instance, in their attempt to promote linen production, the members of the Court encouraged the exchange of flaxseed varieties for crop experimentation. The dissemination and cultivation of different flaxseed varieties led to impressive crop yields. In a report written in 1649,

Beauchamp Plantagenet observed that New Englanders produced more than half a ton of flax and a ton of hemp for each acre sown.[7] In response to official urging, expansion of the provincial sheep flock was rapidly underway within 10 years of settlement. Likewise, the importation of cotton was commonplace. Compelling evidence of the Court's effectiveness was an expanded confidence in textile production by mid-century. Rather than just encourage the work, legislative acts began to require compliance with provincial goals. The Court was neither shortsighted nor foolish. The magistrates firmly believed in the ability of New England towns to abide by their directives.

In the spring of 1656, the General Court notified all Massachusetts Bay households of their new textile policy,

> Not knowing any better ways and means, condusable to our subsis-
> tence, than the improving of as many hands as may be in spinning
> woole, cotton, flax, etc.; It is therefore ordered . . . that all hands,
> not necessarily employed on other occasions, as women, girls, and
> boys, shall be, and hereby are, enjoyned to spin according to their skill
> and ability . . . [8]

Instructing town selectmen to oversee their order, the Court directed towns to identify their potential and actively aspire to the general standards set by their order:

> Every one, thus assessed for a whole spinner, do after this present year,
> 1656, spin for thirty weeks every year three pounds per week of lining,
> cotton, or wooling, and so, proportionately, for one half or one quarter
> spinners.[9]

To enforce the new policy, the Court decided to levy fines on households who did not meet their obligations. For "every pound short," the selectmen were bound to "take special care" to fine the deficient household twelve shillings. Each household was expected to produce its share of the yarn necessary to manufacture the volume of cloth needed to meet the "present straight and necessities that ly upon this country."[10]

The General Court's decision appears to have sparked heated discussion in at least one town meeting. Although the specifics of that debate are now lost, Salem townspeople discussed the possibility of a spinning law at length. William Titcomb, the moderator of the meeting, spoke out against the ordinance and attempted to diminish its power by demoting it to the status of a rumor. Titcomb agreed there had been "much agitation" about a "spinning law," but then denied any such ordinance had been created by the Court. After the meeting, the debate resumed at a local ordinary where Titcomb vehemently denied the existence of such a law. Unfortunately for him, the matter did not end there. Several frustrated men complained to authorities that Titcomb encouraged Salem townspeople to ignore the General Court's enactment. When this charge surfaced at the next town meeting, the selectmen settled the issue by fining Titcomb for "lying" at a public meeting.[11]

Despite whatever misgivings were entertained in Salem, Ipswich leaders rose to the occasion. Adopting a direct approach, the committee "of Seven Men" appointed one selectman to conduct the census in each ward. After the initial count, they compiled a town assessment and calculated the total production quota for each year. In the report presented at a town meeting and copied into the minutes, selectmen estimated that Ipswich possessed the potential to produce 3,870 pounds of finished yarn each year and carefully set out how the obligation would be met by each household.[12]

According to the estimates of the selectmen, more than half of the town's 78 families possessed the ability and resources to produce approximately fifty pounds of yarn per year. At first, this would seem a less than vigorous commitment on the part of the town. Yet, if each household met its quota, Ipswich households had the potential of producing more than 250 yards of fabric per year per house. Given the wardrobe needs of an average family, this level of production was certainly more than enough to satisfy most demands and left a significant surplus.[13] Obviously, a household that exceeded its quota produced surplus fabric available to the local market.

Undoubtedly, Ipswich town selectmen knew the textile needs of an average family well. The original immigrants needed to plan in detail for their initial settlement in New England and at mid-century most selectmen were still first-generation. Their projections, based on commonly held expectations, weighed the work of producing textiles against the labor needed to successfully manage a colonial farmstead. The result was an educated guess as to the volume of textile work that Ipswich families could comfortably sustain. At the same meeting, Ipswich selectmen ordered all single persons within the town to "dispose themselves into service within one month" and become productive members of well-governed families. This was more than just an attempt to bring single people into the ordered life of families; the correspondence of the Court's order and Ipswich's impressment of any supplementary labor was too precise to be just coincidence.[14]

Another element that may have influenced spinning assessments in Ipswich and elsewhere was the availability and distribution of textile tools.

Some, such as scutching boards, scutching knives and flax breaks were simple wooden implements easily made and discarded. Other equipment like spinning wheels, hand cards, hatchels and looms called for varying degrees of joinery and metallurgical skills. Certainly colonial craftsmen had access to examples brought from England to copy and the skill to make new, but this did not mean that every household owned textile equipment. Indeed, probate inventories from the period indicate that many households owned none at all.

This apparent lack of textile equipment lends credence to the argument that imports continued to be the primary source of fabric for New England, even after initial settlement was over. Specifically, historians who support this theory point to a lack of weaving equipment in the colony as a factor in the "deficiency" of textile production. However, a close examination of probate inventories reveals that even though every household did not own a loom, a significant number of looms were available for use in the colony.[15]

Three percent of all Massachusetts probate records sampled in the period report at least one loom and its "appurtenances." No looms were found in Plymouth probate inventories before 1650, but then six percent of the inventories between 1650–1669 contain looms and other weaving equipment. At least one of the Plymouth inventories is attached to a will where two sons inherited equal shares in their father's shop and equipment.[16] In Connecticut's recorded inventories, there were no weavers represented until the third quarter of the century when three weavers are recorded. Since many of the first-generation emigrants lived beyond 1689 and some of their apprentices long into the eighteenth-century, these probate inventories provide only a rough estimate of the number of active weavers at work in New England over the whole period.[17]

Despite the conservative numbers developed from probate inventories, active use of the looms reported produced a substantial volume of cloth. One weaver testified in Ipswich court that he wove an average of 10 yards per day. If a professional weaver spent only 30 weeks a year at his loom and produced at least 60 yards of cloth per week, the gross production would be approximately 140,000 yards of fabric per year.[18]

Another way of gauging the availability of looms to potential weavers is in the response of the Ipswich Quarterly Court to *Hadley vs. Pike*. As we know, Samuel Hadley enlisted the help of his father to sue Joseph Pike for breach of an apprenticeship contract. The litigation between Hadley and Pike exposed more than just a dispute between neighbors, it also illuminated the crucial importance of weaving tools to a newly trained artisan and how important access to new equipment was. Although his apprenticeship was completed, Samuel Hadley could not embark on the journeyman stage of his craft without a loom. His lack of equipment became critical when John Knight offered him his first opportunity to "set up."

Turning to his father, Hadley persuaded him to bring Joseph Pike to court. After hearing the evidence of at least six witnesses and viewing the original indenture document, the Ipswich magistrates found in Hadley's favor. They ordered Pike to pay Hadley's court costs and to provide him with a new loom "with all things fitting for it *within one month* [my emphasis]."

At the least, the judges' decision makes it clear that textile tools were available in Essex County. Hadley could have provided himself with his own loom at his own expense, but because of the contract, he expected Pike to do so. The court agreed, but would not have made such an order without being reasonably sure that Pike could obtain a new loom for Hadley within that time.[19] Although apprenticeship contracts like that of Hadley are rare, those that have survived indicate that master weavers often promised to provide equipment to their apprentices when they completed training. When the master and apprentice were father and son, final ownership of the looms and shop equipment was usually provided by the testamentary documents as in the case of Isaac and Henry Chittenden.[20]

Weavers and their looms were certainly important to the making of cloth, but near the center of the productive network stood the spinners and their wheels. As the basis for yarn production and the grist for the weavers' looms, spinning wheels were also a good indicator of textile tool distribution and activity in the period.

Throughout the period 1630 to 1690, one quarter of Massachusetts' households owned at least one spinning wheel. In comparison, Plymouth and Connecticut households seem to have a similar concentration in the first decade with a greater concentration of tools in Plymouth probates by mid-century. After 1650, Connecticut probate inventories reveal numbers similar to Massachusetts; this indicates a comparable interest in the production of yarns for the weavers across New England. In contrast to the number of looms reported in the inventories, the quantity of spinning wheels seems disproportionate at first. Yet, when one considers that each busy weaver required the yarn output of approximately 20 diligent spinners, the disparity in numbers makes sense. Like the looms of weavers, a spinning wheel could be operated by more than one member of the family or even a neighbor. Thus, one spinning wheel could produce twice or three times the volume of one spinner if there were two or three people to make use of it. Still, spinning wheels were not universally owned and their presence or absence in a household suggests different productive strategies among colonial households.

An analysis of probate inventories organized by wealth discloses a more detailed picture of where spinning wheels were most often found. Households with probate values under £500 were more likely to own spinning wheels than those with greater wealth. This distribution might indicate that households of greater wealth purchased their cloth, imported or locally produced. Another possibility is that middling households, those with probate values between £100–£500, were more typically geared towards artisan/crafts manufacture and could afford to own the tools necessary to the work. Indeed, close analysis of the population of Great Migration immigrants indicate a high percentage were middling craftspeople, some of whom paid to bring their equipment with them.[21] Even if a family did not have access to English-made wheels, provincial craftsmen stood ready to supply the needs of their neighbors. In Massachusetts, two generations of the Pike family (Joseph, b. 1649, and Jeremiah, b. 1673) manufactured spinning wheels in the Framingham area. Their combined work lives spanned almost a century; their spinning wheels were available from the seventeenth into the eighteenth centuries.[22] Thus, locally manufactured wheels could be found in the colonies.

For poorer or younger households, owning equipment was less likely, but access to textile tools could have come through outwork in the neighborhood's wealthier homes. It was spinning that brought Abigail Darling to the Salem Village home of Widow Mary Putnam. She and Deborah Knight, another young woman from beyond Hathorne's Hill, worked together at their wheels and took turns caring for Putnam whose health was rapidly failing. Perhaps because they were sharing nursing duties as well as household chores, both girls were on hand to witness Putnam's will. With her work finished at Widow Putnam's, Abigail returned home for a few days, but quickly moved on to the employ of Goodwife Cheever, a next-door-neighbor of Widow Putnam. Ezekiel and Abigail Cheever needed additional help, since their only daughter was now married and living away. Abigail Darling took her place, at least in front of the Cheever's spinning wheel.[23]

In Andover, as we know, Thomas Barnard employed several young neighborhood women to spin. The children of Barnard's neighbors, the girls undoubtedly knew the family well. Moreover, some of the young women were clearly accustomed to working as a group since they were closely related to each other and probably moved easily between their respective homes. Two of these working women were also sisters: Betsey and Mary Farnum. As the daughters of John Farnum, they were among the Barnards' closest neighbors. Connected by their relationship to Bradstreet and his flock, the Farnum and Barnard families obviously exchanged more than sheep. Three more of the young women, Lydia, Hannah and Mary

Abbott, were the Farnums' first cousins through their mother, Sarah Farnum Abbott.

Not all of the young women were related, though. Bridget Richardson, Dorcas Lacy and Betty Faulkner do not seem to be linked, except by their connection as paid labor to the Barnard household. Thus, economic as well as familial connections influenced who came to the Barnards' home to work.

All of the young women were unmarried at the time and their presence in the Barnard home indicates another way in which textile equipment could be accessed in a community. Surplus daughters could be sent out to work for a neighbor who owned the necessary equipment. Their labor allowed all of the families to share the community's textile production requirements without the investment in equipment that they probably could not afford. At the same time, the girls' wages, figured in money, but likely paid in finished yarn or cloth, provided their parents with access to textiles without cash outlay. By this strategy, families could invest their surplus daughters' labor in the neighborhood textile industry for a tangible return. Only a daughter's marriage interrupted the flow.

At least two of the young women who worked for Barnard wed within five years of his diary notations.[24] Their marriages presumably meant leaving the household of their parents or employers, but did this mean that outwork in the neighborhood would also end? For some women, marriage might mean access to textile equipment through a "setting out" gift from her parents. John Gould, the Topsfield weaver, provided his daughter Phebe a wheel to spin the wool from the three sheep included in her portion.[25] Thus, Phebe Gould had the wool and the wheel to produce yarn in her new husband's home. Another means could have been through marriage to a widower with an already-equipped household, as was the experience of Beatrice Plummer in her second marriage.[26] Under either circumstance, a new wife produced textiles for her own family and possibly had the opportunity to supervise others like Mrs. Barnard. For most, though, access to equipment continued through borrowing and utilizing a neighbor's tools, especially before a couple's first child was born. Even if a young wife had her own wheel, she may still have gone to a neighbor's home to work. As one woman advised her daughter, she "might better do her work an go to another bodys house than they that have a great family can go to hers."[27]

Clearly, the social nature of such gatherings was important to the maintenance of inter-neighborhood relations, but they were a result of the nature of textile production. As we have seen, the making of cloth began with the production of fibers and progressed through stages of processing and spinning before the final weaving and fulling could take place. By the very nature of this complex set of steps, not every household could or would have participated in every step of the process. Instead, some families produced fibers while some processed and created yarns. Other families finished the cloth. At the center of the web of connecting functions there was often a cluster of families that facilitated the productive capabilities of their neighborhood, either by providing tools, skills or some other crucial aspect of the cycle. Reverend Barnard's Andover household operated as just such an anchor in his neighborhood.

We know that Barnard owned a small flock of sheep that produced a substantial wool harvest, especially after the flock was entirely his. He also owned the equipment, at least four spinning wheels and an unspecified number of hand cards, to manufacture wool yarn. To supplement the family's labor needs, Barnard drew on families with surplus daughters and little or no equipment. Yet, despite his impressive network, even Barnard did not produce cloth in his mini-factory. The yarns were sent to the neighborhood weaver and perhaps then on to a local fulling mill before they came back as dressed cloth. Who orchestrated this production? Barnard's account book has an undeniable bias; he never once mentions his wife. So, we have no clear vision of who organized the productive textile work in their home. However, glimpses of other similar webs of production indicate women were more likely to be the stewards of these busy hives.

Margaret Prince, the harassed young matron whose first child was stillborn, participated in just such a female-headed structure. Widow Babson was Prince's near neighbor and actively drew on the immediate community for workers. As a result, Babson's house was perpetually full of neighborhood women like Prince who came and went with fiber, yarn and cloth. At the time of her dispute with William Browne, Prince apparently spun worsted yarn for Babson. As her employer, Babson was the natural authority that Prince appealed to in her distress. Arriving with hands "full of spun wool" for Babson, Prince's entrance was witnessed by no less than five other women, presumably engaged in textile labor. Caught by her labor pains before she could return home, she turned to these women neighbors, along with the local midwife, to deliver her stillborn child and nurse her through recovery.[28]

Another woman who likely coordinated neighborhood skills was Mary Rogers. A native of Yorkshire County England, Mary had grown up in an area that produced fine woolen cloth. As a young woman, she married Ezekiel Rogers, the rector of the parish in Rowley, England. When a parish schism caused the dismissal of her husband from his pulpit, a group of Rowley residents, including Mary and Ezekiel, set out for New England sometime in 1638. This group formed the core of the settlement in Essex County, Massachusetts, known also as Rowley.[29]

When Ezekiel died in 1674, he left an estate that included raw wool, spun yarn and a small flock of sheep. As his widow, Mary was given sole administration of his estate and was entrusted by the court to maintain the value of the estate for their children. Although there was no spinning wheel listed in the inventory, one indication that she drew on neighborhood labor to process her sheep's wool into yarn and then finished cloth were the details of the inventory, which included substantial amounts of raw wool, yarn and cloth. Unfortunately, no testimony like that of Prince's suit against Brown has preserved the details of Mary Roger's network. Yet she may have operated much like Widow Babson. One can easily imagine Mary Rogers distributing her wool to neighborhood spinners, and receiving the spun yarn in return. The raw wool, spun yarn and new wool fabric in her inventory testifies to competent management of her network and it was certainly productive. In the three years following the death of her husband, a neighborhood fulling mill operated by the Pearson family charged Mary Rogers' account for "dressing" more than 35 yards of wool serge. Along the way to the mill, Mary probably traded wool and yarn for the services of the spinners and weaver before the final product of finished fabric came back to her. It is also possible, since the wool clothing in her inventory did not equal the amount of wool fabric that she paid for the spinning and weaving in finished fabric. Mary may well have perpetuated the interdependent circle of production for still another woman when she willed her possessions including her sheep to her cousin, Ann Nelson.[30]

Several characteristics of these women organizers seem to be constant. Babson, Rogers and Putnam were all widows with substantial estates holding various combinations of sheep, cropland, textile tools and access to professional weavers and finishers. Perhaps the other operative factor here was age. Older matrons like Abigail Cheever and Goodwife Barnard operated similar networks, even before their husbands were deceased. With few, if any, younger children in the household, older housewives could turn their attention to the organization of a more complex productive network. With fewer family members to wash, bake and brew for, these women could concentrate vital energy on building equity in their husband's estate, their older children's legacies and making more general wealth available to their household through textiles.

Professional weavers' homes could be centers of production networks as well, though they may well have been overlapping centers in which wives orchestrated yarn production and husbands created fabric. John Gould's workshop produced a variety of fabrics for customers from yarns supplied by his wife and daughter as well as from the members of the productive network associated with his shop. His account book chronicles, if sometimes haphazardly, the interactions of this network.

In one transaction, Gould used flax supplied by "Mr. Symonds" to weave two pieces of cloth for another customer. An uncle's wife spun the dressed flax—a member of Gould's regular laborers—and his apprentice, Benjamin Standly, wove the cloth. In other transactions, Gould arranged for flax to be dressed and prepared for spinning and then passed the flax on to be spun to still another woman. He also owned part of a collectively managed flock of sheep that provided him with a harvest of wool and the basis for some of his wool yarns and cloth.[31]

Textile networks could also develop around a merchant's activities. Since domestic products were the basic currency of most financial transactions of the period, textile products would naturally have come into the hands of merchants. With access to many different households, merchants were in an ideal position to take advantage of the organic development of textile networks and produce finished cloth for sale. Moreover, they could extract additional profit from as many of the different steps of the process they could control. Evidence for this manipulation of the manufacture of domestic textiles can be found in daybooks and ledgers from the period.

The three account books kept by Salem merchant George Curwin during the years 1652–1662 reveal a regular traffic of domestic goods that circulated in and out of his shop. Most of Curwin's accounts were identified with the male head of household's name and noted male goods such as wood or corn by the bushel, but female textile products figured prominently, too. Supplied by housewives or daughters, Curwin sometimes identified their work with notations such as "by your wf's hand." Typically an account's reckoning drew from both male- and female- produced goods such as in the entries for Thomas Dorman that combined fire wood and barrel staves along with spun yarn and honey from his wife's bee hives.[32] One 1659 account, however, shows how the lines between male and female textile-related products could blur.

Headed by a woman's name, Widow Giles, her account reckoned in 1659 lists a bag of raw wool weighing 270 pounds on the credit side. At first glance, one might assume Bridget Giles's transaction to be an unusual case, but this is not so. A widow for almost twenty years, Giles controlled a large meadow, at least 10 acres of arable land and an indeterminate number of livestock. Among her assorted "cattel" she kept a flock of approximately 48 sheep, but with no extant copy of her probate inventory greater detail is impossible. Her wool, traded to Curwin, may have been one of the commodities available to her through her "widow portion" that was meant to be marketable surplus and used as such. Thus, although she had not processed the wool, Widow Giles provided a substantial contribution to the overall production of Salem's textiles and to the personal involvement of George Curwin in its operation.[33]

Curwin's position as a merchant in one of the larger import/export centers of Massachusetts Bay placed him at the nexus of blue water commerce and rural exchange. The pattern of transactions in his account books indicate that he routinely acted as a middleman in the active domestic production of cloth by his customers, especially when it involved the use of imported cotton fibers. Often supplying customers with "cotton woole" on credit, Curwin accepted spun thread and woven textiles as payments on their accounts.[34] The thread and yarn was then parceled out and sold to other individuals who sometimes reconciled their accounts with knitted stockings or woven cloth.

Widow Giles' wool, for instance, as that of other suppliers, was resold to Curwin's customers in smaller amounts usually from six to ten pounds each. These smaller portions of the wool crop came back to Curwin again in the form of woolen yarns and, sometimes, wool fabric. Wool was not the only fiber or yarn type Curwin credited or debited accounts for. Raw cotton, dressed flax, cotton and linen yarns and a variety of fabrics also passed through his accounts. He even profited from the sale of equipment. Curwin's warehouse routinely held multiple pairs of hand cards, sheep shears and knitting needles.[35] Although he may not have been directing the work of a neighborhood as Widow Babson or even Thomas Barnard, George Curwin certainly operated well within the lines of several overlapping circles of production, especially in the Salem area. His scope of business extended beyond Salem, however, partly because of his ready supply of cotton wool. Trading with Barnard and Farnum in Andover, Denison and Knight of Ipswich and Bixby of Topsfield, Curwin benefited at every turn from the productive activities of a great portion of Essex County.

Joshua Buffum handled a similar, though smaller, portion of the textile activity in his mercantile business. The son of an early Salem planter, Joshua inherited two-thirds of his father's land and a woodlot from which he launched his business. From 1674 to 1709, Buffum's account book records the progress of his business with frequent sales of sawn lumber and wooden coffins. However, Buffum did not rely solely on wood for his business. His customers very often settled their accounts with a variety of produce, including textile products. Josia Walcott, for instance, brought Buffum 188 pounds of yarn in November of 1688. Walcott did not bring all of the textile produce of his household to Joshua Buffum. In a pattern related to his personal needs, Walcott brought yarn and knitted stockings to at least two other merchants, Jonathan Curwin and Phillip English.[36]

Buffum, in turn, contributed to this circulation of textile items in a connected series of trades. In some accounts he received yarn for cotton wool. In others, he traded yarn for finished cloth. He may even have rounded out the trade circle by sending his yarn off to the weavers for cloth to sell back to his customers. Between 1692 and 1700, Buffum's accounts reveal an active trade in textile fibers, yarns and cloth of various types. He even seems to have become interested in owning and raising sheep, since he made a meticulous accounting of Salem grazing rights in the "North fold" for 1683, including five "poles" for himself.[37]

A third account book from Connecticut displays a remarkably similar pattern to those of George Curwin and Joshua Buffum. Kept by Peter Berkeley, a merchant with contacts in Barbados, this account book spans the years 1679–1682. Berkeley's ledger carried 19 active accounts kept over several years. Approximately one-quarter of the credits applied to customer accounts were spun fiber, knitted stockings or finished cloth. About half of the purchases included either raw cotton or unspun flax fiber alongside the regular purchases of rum, sugar, salt, and molasses. The pattern of circulation evinced in this ledger closely parallels those of Curwin and Buffum.[38] Fiber, yarn, and cloth circulated from one account to another in an almost perpetual round of production and consumption. The domestic cloth produced in Hartford in this lively exchange may not have moved beyond the limits of the town or even that particular merchant's neighborhood, but certainly contributed to its economic viability.

One final area where the scope and scale of New England's provincial fabric production becomes particularly apparent is in the creation and production of fulling mills. Although fulling was not a necessary step in the creation of all types of cloth, for good wool cloth it was essential. In a fulling process, newly woven wool cloth was washed, shrunk and then felted. Properly dressed cloth was then napped with teasels and evenly sheared for a smooth appearance. The entire process was time consuming, but made the fabric much more valuable. Thus, a serious cloth industry, especially one that produced woolens, required that there were fulling capabilities of some sort available.

The appearance of fulling mills in New England has not been particularly well documented, but there are a few exceptions. A 1635 entry in the Ipswich town records granted John Shatswell a six-acre piece of land on the Egypt River. By 1638, Shatswell acquired two more pieces on the North and Muddy Rivers. Although the town records do not specifically mention his intentions, Shatswell's preference for river sites suggests he was trying to develop an appropriate location for a mill. By 1656, John Shatswell's son,

Richard, operated a hemp mill and shortly thereafter a fulling mill on his father's original six-acre parcel on the Egypt River.[39]

Despite Shatswell's early start in Ipswich, John Pearson built the first documented fulling mill in New England in Rowley, Massachusetts. Not of the original complement of Yorkshire men to come from England, Pearson apparently relocated to Rowley from Salem in 1642 with the intention of erecting a mill. By tradition, Pearson brought the cedar logs for the mill's construction from England, not sure that they would be available in New England. The mill was constructed somewhere on the Mill River near the Bay Road by 1643 at a place that eventually became an industrial complex where logs were sawn, grain made into flour, flax broken and, eventually cloth fulled. Styling himself a clothier, Pearson probably moved to Rowley specifically to take advantage of the townspeople's intention to produce woolen cloth. For the next four generations, Pearson men called themselves clothiers, participated in the operation and expansion of the mill complex and passed the implements of their trade on to their sons.

Another self-styled clothier, Peter Chaney, built a third fulling mill in the town of Newbury close to the Rowley line in 1686. Petitioning the town for permission to set up several types of mill, Chaney promised to build a fulling mill within three years of his occupation of the site. The new mill was obviously meant to complement Pearson's Rowley business because the town's agreement with Chaney expressly connected the operations of the two mills.

> [Chaney] doth engage himself to full this town's cloth before any other
> town's and to do it upon the same terms as Mr. Pearson doth full cloth[40]

Clearly, the town of Newbury wanted a mill enough to give Peter Chaney the land and lumber necessary to build it. Yet, the petition makes clear that the town leaders would not allow Chaney to take advantage of his position in the town. The relative proximity of both mills meant area weavers could expect to get their woolens fulled regardless of the growth in the region's productive capacity.

For more than 40 years until 1730, the Chaney and Pearson families continued to operate their mills in the Rowley/Newbury area. In the meantime, the Pearsons built at least one other fulling mill around 1690 in the area of the first. Later, the entire complex would become known as Byfield mills. Peter Chaney gave his son control of the original mill property and a part interest in the fulling mill in 1694. After the death of his father, Peter Chaney, Jr. sold the entire property to one of John Pearson's grandsons, Jonathan Pearson.[41] From that time on until the early nineteenth-century, the Pearsons retained direct control over all the fulling mills belonging to the original Ipswich and Newbury grants.

The Pearson family's long-term ownership of the Byfield mills complex is significant for its obviously successful employment as a processor of woolens from the Rowley, Newbury and Ipswich towns. John Pearson left a large estate of over a thousand pounds when he died in 1693. Benjamin Pearson, the son who inherited the Byfield mills benefited even more. When he died in 1729, his estate had grown to a value of £2600.[42] Clearly, a considerable volume of domestic textiles flowed through the Pearson mills for them to be so profitable.

Even more important to this study is the survival of at least one of two original account books from the Pearson mills into the twentieth century. The Pearson ledgers, described in detail in *Early Settlers of Rowley, Massachusetts*, documented a significant portion of the cloth that was fulled in the original mill between 1672 and 1689. George Blodgett, an antiquarian and author interested in the history of the Rowley area, did the original analysis of these ledgers.

According to Blodgett, the 16 years covered by the Pearson ledgers he examined included over 618 individual accounts. Virtually every Rowley family had an account (104 families) and another 500 were from towns surrounding Rowley. Over the period covered by the ledgers, the mill purportedly processed 65,000 yards of fine woolen cloth. Unfortunately, the account book described by Blodgett seems not to have survived into the 20th century, but an account book covering the years between 1684 and 1689 has. The second account book, overlapping the first reported by Blodgett and continuing forward another three years, reveals the hive of activity that must have characterized the Pearson mill. In the five years represented in the second account book (some entries carried over from the "old book") Jeremiah Pearson totted up 15,638 yards processed. Over 200 individuals brought their woolen cloth to the Pearson mill for finishing in pieces as small as two yards to lengths as much as 59 yards. Many of the accounts are familiar; the children of Francis Plummer, Amos Stickney and Joseph Pike all fulled cloth at Pearson's mill. If the Pearson mill were the only one in operation, this figure would have been impressive enough, but by the 1670s there were at least two others operating in the Rowley area. Upstream from the main Pearson mill was a separate fulling mill also managed by the Pearson family. In addition, the Shatswell mill operated in Ipswich by this time.

Consider that the 15,638 yards of wool cloth was just a portion of the overall production of fabric. Not all cloth was sent to the mill and certainly not all cloth was sent to the Pearson mill with others nearby. Moreover, in nearly every probate reporting cloth goods, linen outweighed wool cloth by nearly three yards to one. This would mean that if linen, linen/cotton and linsey-woolsey were manufactured in the same proportion as they appear in the probates, nearly 50,000 yards of linen and linen blend fabrics would have been produced over the same time period in just the Rowley area. Clearly, a highly productive system was in place to produce this volume of goods.[43] Across New England this productive system guaranteed that woolen and linen fabrics "of all sorts" rolled off the beams of provincial weavers into the households of their neighbors and communities.

Chapter Five

Good "English" Cloth

"They have many Wool combers, Spin their Wool very fine, of which make some Tammyes, but for their own private use."

—William Harris, 1674[1]

When Edward Taylor imagined his poetic "apparell" and wrote of being "cloathed in Holy robes for glory," it is hard to know if his mind's eye saw English cloth, the work of a neighborhood weaver or his own wife's toil. Certainly his homely metaphor implies a direct familiarity with the process of cloth production; one may assume he equated the laborious tasks associated with making textiles akin to the hard work of living a righteous life.

If Edward Johnson were the poet, the fabric of his "holy robes" would surely be domestic; his spiritual fancy precisely emphasized divine intervention in the success of cloth manufacture in New England. In his view, Jehovah made the flocks of sheep multiply, flax and hemp grow, and gave New Englanders the ability to make good cloth. All of these were the result and the proof of God's purpose for the Saints.

Were Johnson and Taylor's musings mere wishful thinking or did they reflect reality as the two Edwards witnessed it? The passing of more than three centuries obscures the material world inhabited by these two men from present day observers. Seventeenth-century textiles have not survived in large quantities down to the present, especially everyday items. It is no surprise that plain and utilitarian garments did not last. They were worn, repaired, remade and worn again until no longer useful. Then, the pieces were cut up and reused for rug filling, patches, bandages, and the like. Sheets, bed ticking and other utilitarian articles went the same way. Linen rags were recycled as part of the process of papermaking in the seventeenth-century. Fancy goods were less likely to be so completely consumed. Often "best" items were saved for special occasions and became heirlooms rather than mere household "appurtenances." Thus, many of the extant textiles were preserved precisely because they were intrinsically or actually valuable. As a result, people deliberately preserved fancywork rather than utilitarian; given a choice of fancy goods, they probably saved the even more costly imported textiles rather than provincial.

For the purposes of this study, the surviving artifacts of the past are not very instructive. Among the few examples left to us from the seventeenth-century, most represent the "best" rather than the ordinary. Even then, it is not always clear how to separate imported fancy from similar provincial work. One method for winnowing imported from provincial and vernacular examples is the thread density. In general, imported cloth had higher thread counts than the work of provincial weavers and vernacular work had even less.[2] Yet, without provenance, conclusive evidence for the origin of professionally-woven examples is still problematic. More importantly, there are simply not enough extant examples to make definitive judgments concerning the volume and distribution of all three categories in colonial households. Instead, historians must look to the documents— probate inventories, account books and diaries—as the primary source for reconstructing the material life of New England households.

As we have seen, there was never a time when imported fabrics were not available to New Englanders. The first three decades saw substantial quantities of textiles arriving with the immigrants who took part in the Great Migration.[3] Even after the major influx of immigrants ended in the 1640s, trade networks that linked New England, the Caribbean, and England guaranteed that English textiles would still flow across the Atlantic. There is ample evidence that merchants of Salem, Boston, Providence, and Newport as well as lesser-known New England ports regularly purchased, stored and resold English goods, including fabric.

In Salem, Massachusetts, one of those merchants was Phillip English. A prominent merchant and ship-owner, English owned a fleet of over 20 vessels that sailed all over the Atlantic basin.[4] In extant account books, his wealth in trade is clear. Among the casks of rum, hogsheads of sugar and molasses, bags of raw cotton and other sundry Caribbean products, English also carried stocks of English worsted, fine linen and printed calicos. In 1693, a personal inventory of his goods revealed a wealth of clothing made of fine linen, cambric and holland. He sold and personally consumed large quantities of English-made cloth, but not exclusively.[5]

At the same time that Phillip English bought and sold English-manufactured fabrics, he also bought and traded for locally-produced textiles as well. His account books reveal that customers routinely exchanged "cotton woole" for spun thread, wool yarn for knitted stockings and spun linen for linen cloth. In addition he often purchased wool from local farmers and then traded the wool to others who spun it into yarn. He even dealt in textile equipment. "Mr. Clark" purchased a "bag of flax" and a spinning wheel in 1689; later English credited Clark's account with spun thread.[6] Therefore, although Phillip English may have kept a good stock of English and Dutch textiles, he also kept provincial goods alongside them.

Another Salem merchant and shipmaster, William Bowditch, stored imported and provincial fancy textiles together in his warehouse as well. His extensive inventory includes a vast array of "fine" fabrics including fustian, dimity, and broadcloth. In addition there were linen, cotton, and woolen fabrics clearly designated "coarse" and "homemade." According to his probate inventory documents, a spinning wheel, some weaving equipment and hand cards were found among his personal possessions in the "middle garret" of his home. It is possible that his wife, daughters, and possibly their hired girls supplemented his stock of imports with their own work, which he then sold from his shop. Wherever these provincial textiles came from, he clearly traded in both local and imported.

The Bowditch account books, though somewhat disorganized, also reveal a commercial pattern identical to Phillip English. Bowditch's exchange network linked him to England and the West Indies as well as with his neighbors in Salem. Often these transactions overlapped when local goods traded to Bowditch (barrel staves, for instance) became part of a ship's cargo bound for Barbados. There is no direct evidence that that Bowditch traded provincial textiles beyond his Salem business, yet it is likely that domestic cloth found its way into the cargo holds of merchant ships plying the Atlantic coastlines.[7]

A tantalizing hint of textiles exported from New England can be found in the records of John Touzel, another contemporary and business acquaintance of Phillip English. Touzel made frequent visits from New England to Barbados and along the length of the American seaboard to trade. On one voyage he carried 219 gallons of rum, 32 gallons of molasses, 180 gallons of light molasses, 3 Indian handkerchiefs, 73 yards of "onasburg," 33 yards of "bleu linnin," a dozen hats and 2 pair of "womens fine coton stockins." Touzel sailed from New England to Barbados and then back by way of the Carolinas on this voyage. In Barbados, he traded rum for raw cotton while he sold the rest of his personal cargo, including the textiles, in the Carolinas.

The "Indian hankirches" Touzel noted in his book were certainly imported goods, but the "bleu linnin, "onasburg" and the "fine coton stockins" were likely produced in Salem for resale on this voyage. Indeed, the stockings could have been crafted from a store of raw cotton purchased on an earlier voyage. As a very tough utilitarian cloth, the "onasburg" could have been woven to use as packing bags to transport raw cotton. Another common use for this material was slave clothing. Again, given his destinations, "onasburg" would have been a very tradable commodity.

In his notations, John Touzel made distinctions between the different textile items he carried. One fabric was "onasburg" while the other was simply "linnin," even though both items were constructed of linen yarn. Yet, the type of yarn (coarse or fine), the density of the weave (40s up to 60s), the style of the fabric (plain or twill) and the skill of the weaver made a tremendous difference in its penultimate use and its relative value.[8]

A promotional discussion of New England, *New England's First Fruits*, makes specific references to the types of cloth manufactured in New England as "linen, fustians, dimmittees . . . and woolen cloth."[9] At first glance, those four categories would seem to be fairly limited. Yet, within those categories there were endless variables of fiber, thread density, colors and weave quality. More to the point, the account books of weavers reveal that this limited description can hardly describe the range of fabrics produced in provincial workshops. In order to understand the breadth of textile production in New England in the period 1630–1700, cloth must be divided into three main categories: imported, provincial fancy work, and vernacular utilitarian goods.

Imported cloth sold in New England was most often fancy and fine fabric. Holland, dimity, broadcloth, fustian and a host of woolen, linen, and cotton fabrics manufactured by English and Dutch master weavers were common exports to the colonies. In addition, by the third quarter of the seventeenth-century, the East Indies became another source for fine goods, specifically printed calicos, silks and fine cotton muslin. These fabrics were included in the goods that British merchants supplied to their provincial counterparts and evidence of these imported textiles can be found in account books and other documents of coastal New England. Despite the status that imported fabric may have lent to prosperous households, imports were not the only source of fancywork available to colonials.

Indeed, provincial master weavers produced an abundance of fancy cloth that was virtually indistinguishable from many of the fabric styles, weights, and types that arrived from Europe. This is hardly surprising, provincial craftsmen came from the same weaving traditions as their British counterparts. Indeed, many of the first generation weavers in New England trained in old England's workshops. These highly-trained artisans used complex looms with multiple harnesses, capable of producing a wide variety of fabric types from fustians to worsteds. The complexity of their looms could also result in the intricate and elaborate patterns of damask. Their training and equipment allowed them to handle longer warps and produce much finer cloth with higher thread densities. So, provincial master weavers used techniques and equipment identical to their English relatives and likely produced fabrics that were identical. The proof can be found in the account books of professional weavers in the colonies. These records reveal the breadth of provincial expertise.

Consider the evidence in the accounts of Christopher Leffingwell, a Connecticut weaver born in the second half of the seventeenth-century. As a master weaver, he presided over a thriving professional workshop, trained several apprentices and, as we have seen, employed at least one journeyman weaver full time. Although not all of his records have survived, one account book kept between 1697 and 1714 opens a window on his workshop's production for those years. Over that period, Leffingwell, his apprentices, and journeyman produced 15 different types of cloth—everything from "fine napkinning" to sail canvas. The most popular cloth he produced was "fine woolin," presumably a lighter-weight, fulled, wool fabric made from yarns produced locally. Since he distinguished between blanketing, kersey, serge and drugget in his account book, Leffingwell's "fine woolin" cloth was most likely meant for good clothing or bed furnishings. In addition, he wove fancy table linens, patterned bed hangings and "coverlids." These items, both refined and plain, were important in every household—the wealthier households probably commissioned the fancier goods while the modest goods went to lesser homes.

The bed hangings and coverlets produced in Leffingwell's shop reflected his range of clientele. One set of "bed furnishings" cost seven pounds to produce while another set cost less than two. Coverlets could range from two to five pounds and although Leffingwell did not note the reasons for the range in costs, common sense dictates that the complexity of the design and perhaps the quality of the yarns used must have determined the cost. As the master craftsman, Leffingwell would most certainly have been the designer of these pieces and perhaps the weaver, but they do not represent the bulk of the work produced in the shop.

In general, the accounts reveal that Leffingwell produced a broad spectrum of fabric types, especially when compared to his English counterparts. This variety allowed him to draw on the labor of his apprentices as well as his journeyman employee, John Birchard, to keep the looms in motion even if their skill did not approach Leffingwell's. In the employment agreement, Leffingwell hired Birchard to weave "8yds per day of such cloth as is 5d p yard." This was basic fabric, but represented hard work, especially if it was a dense woolen or linen. Indeed, we have a record of some of this work since Leffingwell allowed Birchard to weave for himself "as a part of his wages" to supplement his earnings. Recorded in Leffingwell's account book, Birchard's February 1698 list of work done "for himself" reveals that most of Birchard's weaving was of linen, "striped" and "plain." This plain weave linen (striped or plain) could be used for underclothes, table linens, sheets, bed ticking, pillow covers and so on. Utilitarian by definition, these fabrics were in use in every seventeenth-century English home whether in the colonies or in England.[10]

Another type of specialized fabric woven in Leffingwell's shop, sometimes by Birchard, was sail canvas. In the coastal sea-based economy of New England this is not a surprise. The typical vessel, a ketch, used up to six canvas sails involving many yards of canvas sewn into the appropriate shapes.[11] Yet, weaving sail canvas was a special skill; it may have been Leffingwell's ability to teach that skill that brought Birchard to his shop. A weaver who could produce sail canvas would be in high demand as the shipbuilding and rigging industry expanded at the end of the seventeenth-century.

Leffinwell's account book also reflects the needs of his neighbors. One account is especially revealing of the kind of interaction between Leffingwell and his customers. Between 1697 and 1703, neighbor "Lothrop" commissioned a range of textiles to be woven. In the first year, 21 yards of fine woolen cloth and 8 yards of linen were woven in exchange for "fine hose yarn spun." Over the next six years, Lothrop selected linsey woolsey, kersey, drugget, serge and more "fine" linen and woolen yardage. In all, 113 yards of linen, 110 yards of woolen and 6 yards of linsey-woolsey were listed. In addition, Lothrop commissioned one bed "coverlid." Without more biographical detail, it is impossible to identify Lothrop or to know much about his family, but it seems clear he was either providing clothing or bedding for many children or he was trading his finished cloth with other families. It seems likely that Lothrup was an established farmer, his "credits" were distinctly agricultural. In addition, the Lothrop household seems to have been part of the neighborhood textile network as he brought Leffingwell linen hose yarn. In another entry he supplied a load of firewood. Most telling was the pair of oxen rented to Leffingwell for plowing and a wagonload of turnips—a field crop often used to feed livestock.[12] At first glance, the variety and volume of fabric listed in Lothrop's account seems extensive, but in fact these fabric types represent only one part of his household's needs. Although ranging in weight and composition, the various textiles listed in Lothrop's account with Leffingwell have one striking detail in common—they were meant for clothing and bed furnishings. There are no references to the type of utilitarian fabrics that would have been essential to daily use such as toweling, diaper or tow cloth.

The fine linen woven by Leffingwell for Lothrop may have been sewn into shirts, petticoats or even sheets, but every household needed less fancy goods not represented in the Leffingwell account book. Consequently, although Lothrop acquired an adequate, perhaps even surplus, supply of finer fabrics, he still had to have the mundane sorts to round out his household needs. Although there is no way to know what strategies Lothrop used, it is possible he may have traded some of his finer fabrics for larger amounts of "coarse" ones with a neighbor. Certainly his household possessed the capability to produce yarns, as the Leffingwell account book demonstrates.

While evidence of professional weavers exists in the probate inventories and account books, vernacular weavers are more difficult to document. Often their looms and equipment were bundled in attics and garrets unless in use. Many probate inventories describe "piles of lumber" with weaving tackle laying on top. This indicates that unless the inventory lister knew what a knocked-down loom looked like, they could not identify it. In addition to the impermanent nature of their workplace compared to professional weavers, vernacular weavers produced textiles that were the most utilitarian and simple in design. Yet, these weavers were the mainstays of the neighborhood, producing the kind of basic cloth every household needed.

Many of the vernacular weavers were women. Remember Mary Lawes Neale who, if she had been born a man, might have trained as a master weaver. Instead, Mary and women like her were often relegated to winding quills, spinning warp threads and looking on in their father and husband's workshops. When recruited to weave, they were most frequently trained to do simple, utilitarian weaving.

The typical vernacular weaver was only semi-skilled compared to the master weavers of the colonies. As a rule, they used a very simple balanced loom with two to four harnesses and a limited warp capacity. Yet, these simple tools provided them with the tools necessary to produce much of the basic fabric needs in New England. Imagine Mary warping her father's counter-balanced loom with 38 to 40 yards of linen warp. That would have been the capacity for most simple counter-balanced looms since they lacked moveable warp beams. The density of the fabric would be set with a slay (or reed) of 40 dents and the fabric probably set to standard shirting or sheeting width: 5/4 (45") or 4/4 yards (36") wide.

Mary would commence her work with a linen yarn weft and weave approximately ten yards. This piece, when cut and sewn, would produce a pair of sheets. Each sheet would be a double width of two and a half yards that when hemmed and washed would be approximately 77" in length.

Next, Mary might weave an additional 12 yards with linen weft and use that part of the web to cut and sew two men's shirts as well as two shifts for herself or her daughters. With the remaining 18 yards of warp, Mary could have used a variety of cotton or linen or wool weft to produce winter underclothes, aprons and toweling—all with the same thread density. The fabric could look very different depending on the type of filling (cotton, linen, wool), the weave structure (plain weave or balanced twill), or the use of different colored warp and weft threads to produce stripes and checks.

Mary's decision of what to weave might also be determined by the quality of her warp and weft threads: the best might be used for table linens, with sheets next, shirts and shifts of lesser quality and toweling the least. Yet, all of these garments and articles were fundamentally necessary to housekeeping in this period.[13]

Vernacular weavers did not generally keep account books of their weaving since it was not their business as much as it was a chore amid many in the work life of the typical farming community. However, their work does come to light in the probate inventories and wills of New Englanders. The work of Katharine Fenwick is a case in point. When her husband, George Fenwick, made his will in 1656, he described the fabrics and utensils of a well-appointed home in Saybrook, Connecticut. For instance, he described in detail two "suites" of embroidered bed hangings, one with depictions of "Caesar" and the other of "Diana." He also described a "bed lyned with Sarsnett," "ye Greene imbroydered bed," and a "best bed quilt." His generous legacy to his wife included these items as well as sheets, blankets, furniture, and books. Yet, even as he detailed the textile wealth of *his* household and confidently assigned it to his wife, Fenwick recognized Katherine's work as well. In the midst of the list of items left to her he wrote, "I mention not her Towells, or a bed of her own working, or other things of her owne . . ."[14]

George Fenwick understood the production of those towels and "other things" as peculiarly Katharine's and not in his purview to distribute. While George Fenwick is rare in his recognition, he provides an example of the result and significance of a vernacular weaver whose work supplemented the imported and fancy fabrics of her household. Katherine Fenwick's utilitarian goods ("Towells") and more simple items ("a bed of her own working") were still useful and notable in an otherwise relatively affluent household.[15]

In another Connecticut reference, Joseph Olmstead, a master weaver, credited two of his regular accounts, James Norman and John Pike, with "simple weaving." Norman and Pike paid for the professional work of Olmstead with vernacular work of their own. In addition, Norman and

Pike contributed to the professional weaver's own work with spun yarns no doubt produced in their own homes.[16] These entries underscore a basic element of the provincial textile industry; without the complimentary efforts of vernacular weavers as well as the incredible output of fibers and yarns from their neighbors, professional weavers would not have had viable crafts.

Indeed without the confluence of imported fancy, provincial fancy and provincial vernacular textiles, New Englanders would have suffered. Imports surely supplemented the provincial fancywork and provided a source of less expensive, but good quality cloth while vernacular weavers contributed the mundane fabrics that master craftsmen did not. The availability of all three meant that everyone could acquire basic necessities, even if it meant doing most of the labor. Nowhere can this be better understood than in the probate inventories.

One inventory where this nexus can be plainly seen is that of Hilliard Veren, Jr. In the winter of 1679–80, Veren, a shipmaster and Salem merchant, died on a voyage to Barbados. By April, the Boston County Court had been notified of his death and administration orders granted. The Court ordered Veren's executors to present an inventory at the next Quarterly Court to be held in Salem in June 1680. Between April and June a careful inventory was made and then entered into the Court's records. The surviving inventory reveals that Veren was not just a blue water shipmaster, he was also a land-based entrepreneur who relied on his wife to operate what the listers called a "shop." The inventory of the shop clearly indicates that this was a dry goods business of sorts with an emphasis on fabrics, clothing notions such as buttons, ribbons, needles, and a few other basic household items. The fabric inventory provides an incredible insight into the types of cloth available in Salem, both imported and provincial.

In the shop that Hannah Veren tended, there were approximately fifteen different fabric varieties. Remarkably similar to the list of textiles produced in Christopher Leffingwell's workshop, the most prevalent type of fabric was woolen. In the case of the Veren shop the variety was kersey and within the category of kersey there appears to have been three discrete sub-categories: imported, fine and coarse. The imported kersey in Veren's shop was labeled Irish, valued at three shillings per yard. Another kersey (5 s. per yard) labeled "fine" could have been imported as well. The next sub-category of kerseys were dyed, listed by color and probably produced by local professional weaver. These ranged in value from three to four shillings per yard. Finally, there was a third category of "coarse" kersey listed and valued at two shillings. Clearly, Veren distinguished between what was imported by listing place of origin, but she also distinguished the better provincial cloth from the vernacular. The same valuation pattern occurs in the lists of serge, blanketing, dowlas, and other fabrics in her list. A final similarity between what could be found in the Veren inventory and in Christopher Leffingwell's workshop was sail canvas. Carrying several hundred yards of "narrow" (3/4) and another simply labeled "canvis," Veren obviously catered to the ship rigging industry in Salem.[17] With this new paradigm for understanding the probate inventories, we can now return to Robert Wilkes and Phebe Eaton.

For Wilkes, the heavy wool coat, twill coat, waistcoat and trousers worth about three pounds were probably cut of provincial cloth. That does not mean they were not of good cloth, simply woven locally rather than imported. His cloak, made of broadcloth, could have been fulled at Pearson's mill and most certainly woven in a professional weaver's shop. His "Jackit and britches" could have been made of "coarse carsie," a remnant of this sturdy workman's cloth was listed in his inventory and was most certainly provincial, if not vernacular. A vernacular weaver most likely produced the plain weave linen cloth found in his inventory and valued at 18 d. per yard since it was very inexpensive. His "stockins" could have been made by his sister, Mary Wilkes Woodbery, or purchased from a shop like Hannah Veren's.[18]

For Eaton, her Penniston petticoat could well have been cut from English wool, but her carsee petticoat and "wascutes" as well as the woolen cloth found in her inventory could have come from a provincial source. Indeed, it seems likely, since the valuation of the fabric (4 s. per yard) is very close to the valuation of provincial woolen and kersey available from Phillip English, George Curwin or Hannah Veren. Her "stuffe gound" could also have been made of imported goods while her small lining and cotton petticoat could have come from a neighborhood vernacular weaver. Certainly her uncut four yards of ¾ cotton cloth valued at 15 shillings could have come from either a professional or a vernacular weaver, but since it was not listed as a calico or muslin it was probably not imported.[19]

Both the Wilkes and Eaton inventories illustrate the combinations of imported, provincial fancy and vernacular textiles that can be found in most New England households in the seventeenth-century. A persistence of this pattern into the eighteenth century implies that the provincial system worked well and dovetailed with the imported goods that continued to be available as well. So, although Edward Johnson may have imagined that his "robes of glory" came from the divine workings of a provincial loom, Edward Taylor may not have imagined the same scenario. In fact, Taylor's "robes of glory" could have been of any fine or coarse fabric given that all three would have been visible in his material world.

Notes

NOTES TO THE INTRODUCTION

1. Virginia Anderson, *New England's Generation: The Great Migration and the Formation of Society and Culture in the Seventeenth Century*, (Cambridge: Cambridge University Press, 1991), p. 131.
2. Virginia Anderson, *New England's Generation: The Great Migration and the Formation of Society and Culture in the Seventeenth Century*, p. 132.
3. Bernard Bailyn, *The New England Merchants in the Seventeenth Century*, (New York: Harper and Row, 1964), pp. vii, 75.
4. For a brief discussion of the iron manufacturing of New England, see Bernard Bailyn, *The New England Merchants in the Seventeenth Century*, pp. 62–71.
5. The tradition of English domestic cloth-making was described in Alice Clark, *Working Life of Women in the Seventeenth Century*, (London: George Routledge and Sons, 1919).
6. Sir Anthony Fitzherbert, *Boke of Husbandrye*, 1555, reprinted in Alice Clark, *Working Life of Women in the Seventeenth Century*, pg. 48.
7. Virginia Anderson, *New England's Generation: The Great Migration and the Formation of Society and Culture in the Seventeenth Century*, p. 135–6.
8. Virginia Anderson, *New England's Generation: The Great Migration and the Formation of Society and Culture in the Seventeenth Century*, p. 137.
9. "New England's First Fruits," published in London, 1643, but written in Boston, reproduced in William Bagnall, *The Textile Industries of the United States Including Sketches of Cotton, Woolen, Silk, and Linen Manufactures in the Colonial Period, Volume I, 1639–1810*, (Boston: W.B. Clarke, 1893), pg 6.
10. At this time cotton was used with linen to make blended fabrics. It was very rare to have all cotton fabrics.
11. Bernard Bailyn, *The New England Merchants in the Seventeenth Century*, p. 73.
12. Inventory of Robert Wilkes of Salem, *The Probate Records of Essex County: 1675–1681*, (Salem: The Essex Institute, 1917), (hereinafter *ECPR*), Vol III, pg. 179–180.

13. Inventory of Phebe Eaton of Haverhill, *ECPR*, Vol II, pg. 342–343.

14. Fabric widths were expressed in portions of a yard and cloth width was established at the time of weaving according to the construction of the clothing or other use it was intended. As such, shirting would have been 3/4 (27") wide, sheeting 5/4 (45") and so on. This meant that there would be a minimum of waste when cutting the item out. See Dorothy Burnham, *Cut My Cote,* (Toronto: Royal Ontario Museum, 1977).

15. The sample data were drawn from the probate records between 1655–75 from Massachusetts counties Suffolk and Essex, Plymouth Colony and Rhode Island Historical Documents. The "randomness" of the sample was defined by the fancy of the probate recorders who did not consistently itemize clothing and household goods. *ECPR,* Vol. I & II; *Suffolk County Probate Records,* (hereinafter SCPR) Vol. I & II, *Plymouth Colony Records,* (hereinafter PCR), Vol. I. The population figure for New England was taken from John J. McCusker and Russell R. Menard, *The Economy of British America, 1607–1789,* (Chapel Hill: University of North Carolina Press, 1991), page 103.

16. William Harris, *Rhode Island Historical Collections,* (hereinafter *RIHC*) MSS, X, 147.

17. Virginia Anderson, *New England's Generation: The Great Migration and the Formation of Society and Culture in the Seventeenth Century,* p. 135.

18. Samuel Maverick, *A Briefe Description of New England and the Townes Therein Together With the Present Government,* 1660, reprinted through the Massachusetts Historical Society, (Boston: David Clapp & Son, 1885).

19. In his argument, Bailyn suggests that cloth production persisted in the colony, but only on the fringes and in very minute quantities. In his opinion, the merchants and their extensive trade networks made it possible for colonists to forgo the difficult work and to continue to have the "superior" textiles produced in New England. Bernard Bailyn, *The New England Merchants in the Seventeenth Century,* 74.

20. Edward Taylor, "Huswifery," from Charles Hambrick-Stowe, *Early New England Meditative Poetry,* (Paulist Press), pg. 132.

NOTES TO CHAPTER ONE

1. Captain Edward Johnson, *Wonder-working Providence of Sions Savior in New England,* London, 1654; pg 174, reproduced in *Library of American Civilizations,* microfiche # LAC15925

2. For a detailed discussion of the importance of livestock to the society and economy of New England see Pamela Jean Snow, "Catle, Kine, and Rotherbeasts: Cattle and the plantation of Massachusetts, 1624–1684," MA Thesis, University of Maine, August, 1998.

3. Captain Edward Johnson, *Wonder-working Providence of Sions Savior in New England,* London, 1654, pg 175.

4. John Higgenson, Connecticut Historical Society, *Collections,* III, 319.

5. The average ewe produced at least one lamb each season and lived to approximately 10 years. Since many ewes produced twins, a reasonable estimate of lifetime production is 15 lambs in 10 years. This means that each flock had the potential to more than double in size each lambing season. Even a more conservative estimate of one lamb per birth means that the flock can still come close to doubling its size in one season.

6. Higgenson's estimate must have been accurate since at the end of the century the sheep flocks in Rhode Island numbered over two hundred thousand. La Mothe Cadillac, Maine Historical Society, Collections, VI, 288.

7. Modern wool breeds produce 10 to twelve pounds of fleece a year, but according to an eighteenth-century farm manual, the average yield among most English longwool breeds in 1780s was about four pounds. This was before bringing in the Spanish merino which considerably increased wool yields in the early nineteenth century. I have settled on an estimate of four pounds yielded per year owing to the feed quality differences between England and New England in this period.

8. The town of Charlestown collectively owned 400 head of "great cattell" as well as "near about 400 sheape." Captain Edward Johnson, *Wonder-working Providence of Sions Savior in New England*, London, 1654, pp. 41, 175.

9. Order of Massachusetts Bay General Court, May 14, 1645, reproduced in William Bagnall, *The Textile Industries of the United States Including Sketches of Cotton, Woolen, Silk, and Linen Manufactures in the Colonial Period, Volume I, 1639–1810*, pg 6.

10. Order of Massachusetts Bay General Court, August 22, 1654, Nathaniel Shurtleff, ed., *Records of the Governor and Company of the Massachusetts Bay in New England*, (Boston: M. White, 1853–4), Volume IV.

11. A wether is a castrated ram. There are several reasons why rams were castrated. First, to control breeding too close to the flock's bloodline, ram lambs were castrated to prevent them from mating with their offspring. Second, rams, especially during the breeding season will fight for dominance and castrating subdues this tendency. Third, castrating boosts production of wool since the energy deflected from hormonal and breeding activity goes into other areas of growth, especially in wool.

12. Account book of Samuel Ingersol, 1685–1695, Mss 21, Peabody Essex Museum, Phillips Library, Salem, Massachusetts. Ingersol recorded several sales of sheep while he was engaging in a Barbados–New Foundland regular shipping route. The values recorded were substantially higher than those in general probates at the same time. I am assuming that he was getting premium for them because they were a lucrative cargo.

13. Order of the Connecticut General Assembly, Colonial Records of Connecticut, Vol. I, pg. 349; Vol. II, pg. 34, 51, 139.

14. Order of Massachusetts Bay General Court, May 14, 1645, reproduced in William Bagnall, *The Textile Industries of the United States Including Sketches of Cotton, Woolen, Silk, and Linen Manufactures in the Colonial Period, Volume I, 1639–1810*, pg 6.

15. Abiel Holmes, D.D., *The Annals of America from the Discovery by Columbus in 1492 to the year 1826,* (Cambridge: Hilliard and Brown, 1829), Volume I, pg 474.

16. Captain Edward Johnson, *Wonder-working Providence of Sions Savior in New England,* London, 1654; pg. 208.

17. *Plymouth Colony Records,* Vol. I & II, Wills and Inventories, ed. C.H. Simmons, Jr., (Maine: Picton Press, 1996).

18. For a survey of early Massachusetts laws and General Court orders relating to cloth production see William Bagnall, *The Textile Industries of the United States Including Sketches of Cotton, Woolen, Silk, and Linen Manufactures in the Colonial Period, Volume I, 1639–1810.*

19. Entry dated April 25th, 1657, Ipswich Town Records, 1634–1662, Manuscript #21, leaf 1, Peabody Essex Museum, Salem, Massachusetts.

20. Entry dated January 5, 1639, Ipswich Town Records, 1634–1662, Manuscript #21, leaf 1, Peabody Essex Museum, Salem, Massachusetts. Will of William Fellows, March 27, 1677, *ECPR,* Vol. III, pg. 128–130.

21. Entry December 12, 1658, Ipswich Town Records, 1634–1662, Manuscript #21, Peabody Essex Museum, Salem, Massachusetts. The "fold" described in this entry is most likely an enclosure made with high, solid wooden fences meant to keep the sheep flock closely under supervision for the night. Sometimes, the enclosure would be partially roofed over to provide shelter from rain as well. Very often the shepherds would make a temporary residence for themselves right up against the fold's walls, so they were readily available if anything threatened the safety of the flock, especially the younger lambs.

22. Entry dated April 25th, 1657, Ipswich Town Records, 1634–1662, Manuscript #21, leaf 1, Peabody Essex Museum, Salem, Massachusetts.

23. These standards are still accepted wisdom today. For early modern England see Thomas Tusser, *Five Hundred Points of Good Husbandry,* 1580 edition reproduced, (London: Lackington, Allen & Co, 1812), pg. 149. For seventeenth century Massachusetts see Marblehead Town Records, *Essex Institute Papers,* Vol. LXIX, No. 3–4,(July–October, 1933):207–329.

24. A "gate" was another form of measure for the common pastures. In Rowley, a gate was equivalent to one acre by order of the town selectmen, 25 February 1662, Rowley Town Records, (Rowley, Massachusetts: 1894), pg. 129.

25. Will of Francis Lambert, *ECPR,* Vol. I, pg. 94.

26. Will of John Lambert, *ECPR,* Vol. II, 102–3.

27. Guardianship of Abigail Lambert, *ECPR,* Vol. III, pg. 426.

28. Will of Reverend Ezekiel Rogers, *ECPR,* Vol. I, pg. 331–6.

29. Will of William Stickney, *ECPR,* Vol. II, pg. 5–8.

30. Salem Town Records, Vol. 1–3, 1634–1691, reproduced in *Library of American Civilizations,* microfiche # LAC20507.

31. Robert Lord is listed as a clerk and a marshal on several probate records recorded in Essex County, Salem Quarterly Court Records, Vol. 6 leaves 6, 13. Entry for February 5, 1650, Ipswich Town Records, 1634–1662, Manuscript #21, Peabody Essex Museum, Salem, Massachusetts.

32. *Marblehead Town Records,* Volume 1, 1648–1683, (Salem: Essex Institute, 1933).

33. *Salem Town Records,* Vol 1–3, 1634–1691, reproduced in *Library of American Civilizations,* microfiche #LAC20507

34. Jared Eliot, *Essays Upon Field Husbandry in New England, As It Is Or May Be Ordered,* (Boston: Edes and Gill, 1762), pg 8.

35. Sarah Knight, *The Journal of Madame Knight,* (reprinted in New York: Peter Smith, 1935), pg 62.

36. Entry dated November 17, 1659, Ipswich Town Records, 1634–1662, Manuscript #21, Peabody Essex Museum, Salem, Massachusetts.

37. Reported in Carl Bridenbaugh, *Fat Mutton and Liberty of Conscience,* pg. 55.

38. Barnard recorded only one loss of a lamb to the wolves.

39. Manuscript Diary of Reverend Thomas Barnard, 1688–1707. Family Manuscript Collection, #B2598, Peabody Essex Museum, Salem, Massachusetts.

40. *PCR,* Vol. II, Part I, pg. 36–38.

41. Will of Hugh Alley, Sr., *ECPR,* Vol. II, (Salem: The Essex Institute, 1917), pg 407–408.

42. Account Book, John Gould of Topsfield (1662–1724), Mss 223, Peabody Essex Museum Library, Salem, Massachusetts.

43. I developed the typical cost of a breeding ewe by averaging probate values from the period. *ECPR,* Vol. I, II, & III. *SCPR,* Vol. I–IX, unpublished microfilm. PCR, *Vol. I & II. CRC, 1635–1669. Digest of Early Connecticut Probate Record.* For another source that confirms my estimates, see Louis G. Connor, *A Brief History of Sheep Industry in the United States,* (Washington, D.C.: GPO, 1921), pg 93.

44. Jeanne Boydston, *Home and Work: Housework, Wages, and the Ideology of Labor in the Early Republic,* (New York: Oxford University Press, 1990), pg. 5–9.

45. Thomas Tusser, *Five Hundred Points of Good Husbandry,* (1580), pg. 149.

46. Gelding was the process of emasculating ram lambs by binding the scrotum tightly enough to destroy the testes and render the animal incapable of reproduction. Docking was the practice of removing the tails by chopping them off with a hatchet and then dipping the severed end in tar to prevent disease.

47. Thomas Tusser, *Five Hundred Points of Good Husbandry,* (1580),pg. 271.

48. Quoted in Alice Clark, *Working Life of Women in the Seventeenth Century,* pg. 62.

49. In England, the strolling poor would send their children out to gather wool left on hedges by the sheep in the spring before they were sheared. See Alice Clark, *Working Life of Women in the Seventeenth Century.*

50. Letter from Dorothy Osborne to Sir William Temple, 1652–1654, reprinted in Alice Clark, *Working Life of Women in the Seventeenth Century,* pg. 54.

51. Entry December 12, 1658, Ipswich Town Records, 1634–1662, Manuscript #21, Peabody Essex Museum, Salem, Massachusetts. John Payne Probate Inventory, *ECPR,* Vol.III, pg 177–178.

52. Marcus Rediker, "Good Hands, Stout Heart, and Fast Feet: The History and Culture of Working People in Early America," *Labour/ Le Travailleur,* 10 Autumn 1982), 123–144.

53. Most hats not made of beaver skin felt or summer straw were made from wool felt.

54. Family papers of George Curwin, 1610–1684, Mss 45, Peabody Essex Museum, Phillips Library, Salem, Massachusetts.

55. Entry of November, 1693, Manuscript Diary of Reverend Thomas Barnard, 1688–1707. Family Manuscript Collection, #B2598.

56. Mary Rowlandson's account can be found in Charles H. Lincoln, ed., *The Narratives of the Indian Wars, 1675–1699,* (New York: Charles Scribner's Sons, 1913), pp 149–61.

57. These were the wool fabrics most often mentioned in probate inventories in the period.

58. Florence M. Montgomery, *Textiles in America, 1650–1870,* (New York: W.W.Norton, 1984), pp. 177–9.

59. William Bagnall, *The Textile Industries of the United States Including Sketches of Cotton, Woolen, Silk, and Linen Manufactures in the Colonial Period, Volume I, 1639–1810,* pg. 12.

60. Report from Caleb Heathcote to the 1703 Royal Council on Foreign Trade. See William Bagnall, *The Textile Industries of the United States Including Sketches of Cotton, Woolen, Silk, and Linen Manufactures in the Colonial Period, Volume I, 1639–1810,* pg. 12.

NOTES TO CHAPTER TWO

1. Captain Edward Johnson, *Wonder-working Providence of Sions Savior in New England,* London, 1654; pg 174.

2. "New England's First Fruits . . . ,"(1643), reprinted in *Collections,* Vol. 1–70, (Cambridge: Massachusetts Historical Society, 1792–1915), pp. 242–250.

3. There are two types of linen fibers that are spun. The long fibers are spun into line yarn and the short fibers spun into tow yarn. The tow yarn tended to be used in the most utilitarian items.

4. For a discussion of seventeenth-century costume, see Patricia Trautman, "Dress in Seventeenth-Century Cambridge, Massachusetts: An Inventory-Based Reconstruction," in *The Dublin Seminar for New England Folklife Annual Proceedings, 1987,* ed. Peter Benes, (Boston: Boston University, 1989):51–73.

5. Quoted in Florence M. Montgomery, *Textiles in America, 1650–1870,* pg. 244.

6. James K. Hosmer, *Winthrop's Journal,* 1630–1649, (New York: 1903), Vol. II, pg. 328.

7. Florence M. Montgomery, *Textiles in America, 1650–1870,* pg. 244–245.

8. Quoted in Florence M. Montgomery, *Textiles in America, 1650–1870,* pg. 218–222.

9. General Assembly order dated 8 February, 1641, reprinted in William Bagnall, *The Textile Industries of the United States Including Sketches of Cotton, Woolen, Silk, and Linen Manufactures in the Colonial Period, Volume I, 1639–1810*, pg. 5.

10. Inventory of Mahalaleel Munnings, Town of Boston, *SCPR*, Vol. III, pg. 229.

11. Account books of George Curwin, Volume 1–3, 1652–1662, Mss 45, Peabody Essex Museum, Phillips Library, Salem, Massachusetts.

12. Estate Inventory of George Curwin, Box 9, Folder 5, Mss 45, Peabody Essex Museum, Phillips Library, Salem, Massachusetts.

13. Letter to Daniel and Robert Hooper, 08-12-1700, Francis Ellis Manuscript, letterbook, Peabody Essex Museum, Phillips Library, Salem, Massachusetts.

14. All of the letters pertaining to this voyage are contained in one small letterbook. The price of the goods were noted in the margins of the letters. Letterbook, Francis Ellis Manuscripts, Peabody Essex Museum, Phillips Library, Salem, Massachusetts.

15. Samuel Ingersol Account Book, 1685–1695, Mss 21, Peabody Essex Museum, Phillips Library, Salem, Massachusetts.

16. March 1694 entry, Memorandum to Joseph Grow from William Gedney. Samuel Ingersol Account Book, 1685–1695, Mss 21, Peabody Essex Museum, Phillips Library, Salem, Massachusetts.

17. PCR, Vol. II, 454–458.

18. Letter to Samuel Taylor, Box 1, file 1, item 2, Barton Family Manuscripts, Mss 110, Peabody Essex Museum, Phillips Library, Salem, Massachusetts.

19. Edward Hunt to Robert Barker, Case 132, Volume 1, Records and Files of the Quarterly Courts of Suffolk County, unpublished microfilm, University of Massachusetts Library, Amherst, Massachusetts.

20. Joshua Buffum account book, 1674–1704, Buffum Family Manuscripts, FMS B9293, Peabody Essex Museum, Phillips Library, Salem, Massachusetts.

21. Account book of George Curwin, Volume 2, 1655–1657, Mss 45, Peabody Essex Museum, Phillips Library, Salem, Massachusetts.

22. Account book of Peter Berkeley, Connecticut Historical Society, West Hartford, CT.

23. The cotton fibers imported from Barbados and the West Indies was of the Sea Island variety that contained fewer seeds and lacked the sticky film that made mainland cotton so difficult to process before Eli Whitney's cotton gin.

24. Rolls are the long narrow rolls of cotton or wool that were "rolled" off the hand cards. They would keep their shape and could be stacked away until needed. When brought out for spinning, the hand-sized rolls were easily picked up and spun by starting the fibers onto the spindle from one end.

25. Although probate inventories report the existence of "cotton wheeles," it is not clear whether they were originally produced for the purpose of spinning cotton. Given the relatively new introduction of cotton in England as well as New England, it may be that spinners merely altered their wheel ratios, cotton needs to be spun more slowly, by changing the size of the pulleys operating the wheel's spindle.

26. See A.P. Wadsworth and Julia D.L. Mann, *The Cotton Trade and Industrial Lancashire, 1600–1780,* (Manchester: Manchester University Press, 1931).

27. Frame knitting was already well-established in England by this period and tradition has it that Ipswich was a center of lace making and then frame knitting in the 17th- and early eighteenth-century based on the theft of knitting frames by men wanting to import the technology. Ipswich could very well have been following Boston's lead, a place to which many Ipswich people had close ties. Both industries are mentioned in Thomas Franklyn Waters, *Ipswich in the Massachusetts Bay Colony,* (Ipswich: Ipswich Historical Society, 1905).

28. The average linen sheet was made from approximately five yards of linen. The fabric was cut into two two-and-a-half-yard lengths and the two pieces were then sewn lengthwise together into a double width.

29. Thomas Tusser, *Five Hundred Points of Good Husbandry,* (1580), pg. 172.

30. Will of John Dresser, Sr., *ECPR*, Vol II, pg. 262–265.

31. Will of John Balch, *ECPR*, Vol I, pg. 96–97.

NOTES TO CHAPTER THREE

1. Sampler, worked by Loara Standish, circa 1640–50, Plymouth Hall Museum, Plymouth, Massachusetts.

2. Virginia Anderson, *New England's Generation: The Great Migration and the Formation of Society and Culture in the Seventeenth Century,* p. 134. See also Roger Thompson, *Mobility and Migration: East Anglian Founders of New England, 1629–1640,* (Amherst: University of Massachusetts Press, 1994).

3. For English women and textile skills, see Alice Clark, *Working Life of Women in the Seventeenth Century.*

4. Virginia Anderson, *New England's Generation: The Great Migration and the Formation of Society and Culture in the Seventeenth Century,* p. 136–137.

5. Edward Johnson, *Wonder-working Providence of Sions Savior in New England,* (London, 1654), p. 130; reproduced in the Library of American Civilizations, microfiche # LAC15925.

6. John Demos, *A Little Commonwealth: Family Life in Plymouth Colony,* (Oxford: Oxford University Press, 1970), p. 185.

7. Daniel Vickers, *Farmers and Fishermen: Two Centuries of Work in Essex County, Massachusetts, 1630–1850,* (Chapel Hill: University of North Carolina Press, 1994), p. 64.

8. *SCPR*, unpublished microfilm, Volume III, p. 106–8.

9. For a good discussion on parental obligations, see John Demos, *A Little Commonwealth: Family Life in Plymouth Colony,* p. 104–105.

10. Recounted in John Demos, *A Little Commonwealth: Family Life in Plymouth Colony,* p. 120–121.

11. The only record of Mary Killam is her "putting out." Judd Manuscript, Massachusetts Miscellaneous Collection, Vol. 14, p. 233, Forbes Library Special Collections, Northampton, Massachusetts.

12. Laurel Thatcher Ulrich, *Good Wives: Image and Reality in the Lives of Women in Northern New England, 1650–1750*, (New York: Alfred a. Knopf, 1982), p. 29.

13. Spinning wages in this period were approximately 2 shillings per pound for worsted or linen yarn and half a crown per pair of stockings. See J. Leander Bishop, *A History of American Manufactures*, (Philadelphia: E. Young and Son, 1868), Vol. I, p. 317–319. For Barnard material see Barnard Family Papers, Reverend Thomas Barnard, 1688–1707, Mss FMS B2598, entry dated November 1693, Peabody Essex Museum Library, Salem, Massachusetts.

14. Estate of Renold Foster, Sr., *ECPR*, Vol. III, p. 419–422.

15. Account book, John Gould of Topsfield (1662–1724), Mss 223, p. 5–7, Phillips Library, Peabody Essex Museum, Salem, Massachusetts.

16. Paul Boyer and Stephen Nissenbaum, ed., *The Salem Witchcraft Papers: Verbatim Transcripts of the Legal Documents of the Salem Witchcraft Outbreak of 1692*, (New York, 1977), Vol. III, p. 678.

17. In an entry dated April 2, 1686, Mary Walcott's father credited his account with over thirty pounds of spun yarn. In another entry, he brought five pairs of knitted stockings. Phillip English Account book fragment, English–Touzel–Hathorne Papers, 1665–1690, Mss 11 Box 17, folder 3, Phillips Library, Peabody Essex Museum, Salem, Massachusetts.

18. Paul Boyer and Stephen Nissenbaum, ed., *The Salem Witchcraft Papers: Verbatim Transcripts of the Legal Documents of the Salem Witchcraft Outbreak of 1692*, (New York, 1977), Vol. III, p. 683.

19. *The Salem Witchcraft Papers: Verbatim Transcripts of the Legal Documents of the Salem Witchcraft Outbreak of 1692* Vol. III, pg. 683.

20. Trial of Winifred Holman, Middlesex County Superior Court Folio Collection, old folio 25, Massachusetts Archives, Columbia Point, Boston, Massachusetts.

21. *Records and Files of the Quarterly Courts of Essex County, Massachusetts,* (Salem: Essex Institute, 1912–75), Vol. II, p. 37–8.

22. In a sample of 151 identified artisans who emigrated in the 1630s, 24 of them were weavers. See Roger Thompson, *Mobility and Migration: East Anglian Founders of New England, 1629–1640*, (Amherst: University of Massachusetts Press, 1994), p. 82–91.

23. Census taken from *ECPR* and *SCPR* where occupations were reported either by decedent in a will or by inventory clerks in the probate records.

24. *PCR*, pg. 248, 419–421, 432, 467, 482–485.

25. Charles Manwaring, *A Digest of the Early Connecticut Probate Records*, (Hartford: R. S. Peck & Co. Printers, 1904); CRC, 1635–1665.

26. Carl Bridenbaugh, *Fat Mutton and Liberty of Conscience*, p. 77.

27. William Bagnall, *The Textile Industries of the United States Including Sketches of Cotton, Woolen, Silk, and Linen Manufactures in the Colonial Period*, (Boston: W.B. Clarke, 1893), Vol. I, p. 8.

28. Ipswich Town Records, Volume II, Entry 22 December, 1671, p. 332.

29. Ipswich Town Records, various entries, Volume I, p. 328, 348; Volume II, p. 39, 60, 87, 162, 210, 329, 330.

30. *ECPR*, Vol. I–III. *SCPR*, Vol. I–IX.
31. Although there is no extant inventory of Payne's property, the detail of his will makes it clear that Payne's estate was worth at least £200 and probably more. Will of Thomas Payne, *ECPR*, Vol. I, p. 37.
32. Plummer's estate value was £412. Estate of Francis Plummer, *ECPR*, Vol. II, p. 319–322.
33. Inventory and proofs of John Kingsbery, *ECPR*, Vol. II, pg. 224–225; III, pg. 222.
34. In her testimony before the Salem Quarterly Court, Abigail White described how Edmund Berry constantly derided his wife, Bettorice Berry, in White's presence, even when Bettorice performed tasks helpful to him such as winding his quills. *Records and Files of the Quarterly Courts of Essex County, Massachusetts*, Vol. VI, p. 194–196.
35. Will of Thomas Chittenden, 7 October, 1668, *PCR*, pg. 482–484.
36. William P. Upham, "Records of Salem, 1634–1659," *Essex Institute Historical Collections*, 2nd Series, Vol. I, No. 1 (1868), 59.
37. For Lawes details see Virginia Anderson, *New England's Generation: The Great Migration and the Formation of Society and Culture in the Seventeenth Century*, p. 33n, 116, 117, 138n; Roger Thompson, *Mobility and Migration: East Anglian Founders of New England, 1629–1640*, p. 87, 93, 118, 233; *ECPR*, Vol. II, p. 49–52. For John Neale, Jr. see *ECPR* Vol. III, p. 342–344.
38. Will of Robert Mansfield and Inventory of Mary Lawes Mansfield, *ECPR*, Vol. II, p. 275–279.
39. Inventory of Samuel Mansfield, *ECPR*, Vol. III, 306–307.
40. Will of William Stickney, *ECPR*, Vol. II, p. 6.
41. Will of Amos Stickney, *ECPR*, Vol. II, p. 242–244.
42. Lemuel Abijah Abbott, *Descendants of George Abbott, of Rowley, Massachusetts*, (n.p., 1906), p. 76.
43. The 1664 indenture was recopied into the court record by the clerk. *Records and Files of the Quarterly Courts of Essex County, Massachusetts*, (Salem, Massachusetts: 1913–1921), March 1670, p. 219n
44. Testimony of Thomas Haynes and Mary Holten, *Records and Files of the Quarterly Courts of Essex County, Massachusetts*, March 1670, p. 219n.
45. William Bagnall, *The Textile Industries of the United States Including Sketches of Cotton, Woolen, Silk, and Linen Manufactures in the Colonial Period*, Vol. I, p. 8.
46. Christopher Leffingwell Account Book, 1698–1714, Connecticut Historical Society Archive, West Hartford, CT.

NOTES TO CHAPTER FOUR

1. Edward Johnson, *Wonder-working Providence of Sions Savior in New England*, pg 130.
2. John Demos, *A Little Commonwealth: Family Life in Plymouth Colony*, p. 183.

3. Laurel Thatcher Ulrich, *A Midwife's Tale: The Life of Martha Ballard Based on Her Diary, 1785–1812,*(New York: Alfred A. Knopf, 1990), p. 78–9.

4. Order of the Massachusetts Bay General Court, May 13, 1640, Records of the Governor and Company of the Massachusetts Bay in New England, Nathaniel Shurtleff, ed., (Boston: 1853), Volume I, p. 294.

5. Order of October 7, 1656, Records of the Governor and Company of the Massachusetts Bay in New England, Volume I, p. 294.

6. William Bagnall, The Textile Industries of the United States Including Sketches of Cotton, Woolen, Silk, and Linen Manufactures in the Colonial Period, Vol. I, p. 5.

7. Plantagenet was quoted in J. Leander Bishop, History of American Manufactures, (Philadelphia: E. Young & Company, 1868), p. 316.

8. Order of May 30, 1656, Records of the Governor and Company of the Massachusetts Bay in New England, Volume I, p. 303.

9. Order of May 30, 1656, Records of the Governor and Company of the Massachusetts Bay in New England, Volume I, p. 303.

10. First Section, Order of May 30, 1656, Records of the Governor and Company of the Massachusetts Bay in New England, Volume I, p. 303.

11. William Titcomb case, Records and Files of the Quarterly Courts of Essex County, Massachusetts, WPA transcripts, Vol. III, p. 116–117.

12. Entry December 10, 1656, Ipswich Town Records, Volume I, folio 199, Ipswich Town Clerk, Ipswich, Massachusetts.

13. This estimate is based on the average wardrobes for men and women discussed in the introduction and an average family consisting of seven children and two adults. For family size see Philip J. Greven, Jr., "Family Structure in 17th-century Andover," in Colonial America: Essays in Politics and Social Development, Stanley Katz and John Murrin, eds., (New York: Alfred A. Knopf, 1983):142–161. Greven observes the parallel numbers in several other community studies in his article.

14. Entry December 10, 1656, Ipswich Town Records, Volume I, folio 198, Ipswich Town Clerk, Ipswich, Massachusetts.

15. Looms are not complex in their construction and some very fine joinery was being done in the two counties during the period. At least one very elaborate tape loom was constructed in Ipswich by Thomas Dennis in the 1660s. See Helen Park, "Thomas Dennis, Ipswich Joiner: A Re-examination," Antiques, LXXVII (July, 1960):40–44 and "The Seventeenth-Century Furniture of Essex County and Its Makers," Antiques, LXXVII (October, 1960):350–55. See also Dean A. Fales, Essex County Furniture: Documented Treasures from Local Collections, 1660–1860, (Salem: Essex Institute, 1965), plate 11.

16. PCR, Vol. II, pg. 482–484.

17. In an informal survey of quarterly court records and town histories, I have identified at least 30 additional Essex County weavers who survived past 1700.

18. This figure assumes that all of the households had only one loom and one weaver that worked about 180 days a year. It is actually a conservative

figure since some shops, like that of Thomas Payne or Thomas Chittenden, had more than one loom and many households had more than one resident weaver.

19. George Hadley vs. Joseph Pike, Records and Files of the Quarterly Courts of Essex County, Massachusetts, Vol. IV., p. 218–220.

20. Records and Files of the Quarterly Courts of Essex County, Massachusetts, Vol. I:90; Vol. IV:218–220; Vol. V:159, 202, 389. PCR, Vol. II, Pg. 482–484.

21. See Virginia Anderson, New England's Generation: The Great Migration and the Formation of Society and Culture in the Seventeenth Century, (Cambridge: Cambridge University Press, 1991); Roger Thompson, Mobility and Migration: East Anglian Founders of New England, 1629–1640, (Amherst: The University of Massachusetts Press, 1994).

22. See Hamilton Hurd, History of Middlesex County, Massachusetts, Volume III, (Philadelphia: J.W. Lewis & Co., 1890), p. 643.

23. Paul Boyer and Stephen Nissenbaum, ed., Salem-Witchcraft: A Documentary Record of Local Conflict in Colonial New England, p. 220–1.

24. A marriage for Betsey Farnum to George Holt was recorded on 10 May, 1698. See Clarense Almon Torrey, New England Marriages Prior to 1700, (Baltimore: Genealogical Publishing Company, Inc, 1985), p. 385.

25. John Gould Account Book, Mss 233, Box 1, Folder 1, leaf 75, Phillips Library, Essex-Peabody Museum, Salem, Massachusetts. Sylvestor Judd recorded the "setting out" list of Sarah Wright (Hadley) that also included two spinning wheels. Judd Miscellaneous Manuscript, Vol. i, p. 91.

26. Laurel Thatcher Ulrich, Good Wives: Image and Reality in the Lives of Women in Northern New England, 1650–1750, (New York: Alfred a. Knopf, 1982), p. 29.

27. Records and Files of the Quarterly Courts of Essex County, Massachusetts, Vol. III, p. 140.

28. Records and Files of the Quarterly Courts of Essex County, Massachusetts, Vol. II, pp. 37–8. WPA transcript, Phillips Library, Peabody Essex Museum, Vol. III, pp. 108–113.

29. Edward Johnson, Wonder-working Providence of Sions Savior in New England; George Brainard Blodgett, Early Settlers of Rowley Massachusetts, (Rowley: Amos Everette Jewett, 1933), p. 273.

30. Inventory of Ezekiel Rogers, ECPR, Vol. II, pp. 416–417; Will and Inventory of Mrs. Mary Rogers, Vol. III, pp. 289–291.

31. John Gould Account Book, Mss 233, Box 1, Folder 1, Phillips Library, Peabody Essex Museum, Salem, Massachusetts.

32. Family Papers of George Curwin, 1610–1684, Mss.45, George Curwin Account Book, Volume III, p. 33, Peabody Essex Museum Library, Salem, Massachusetts.

33. Family Papers of George Curwin, 1610–1684, Mss.45, George Curwin Account Book, Volume III, p. 22, Phillips Library, Peabody Essex Museum Library, Salem, Massachusetts.

34. Family Papers of George Curwin, 1610–1684, Mss.45, George Curwin Account Book, Volume I, II & III, Peabody Essex Museum Library, Salem, Massachusetts.

35. Loose papers associated with George Curwin's accounts, Curwin Family Papers, Box 9, item 6, Phillips Library, Peabody Essex Museum Library, Salem, Massachusetts.

36. Fragment of Jonathan Curwin Account Book, Curwin Family Papers, Box 9; Phillip English Account Book, English–Touzel–Hathorne Papers, Box 17, folder 3, Phillips Library, Peabody Essex Museum Library, Salem, Massachusetts.

37. Robert Buffum Estate, ECPR, p. 174–177; Joshua Buffum Account Books, 1674–1709, FMS B9293, Phillips Library, Peabody Essex Museum, Salem, Massachusetts.

38. Account Book, Peter Berkeley, Connecticut Historical Society, West Hartford, CT.

39. Ipswich Town Records, I:3, 7, 9, 11, 207.

40. Pearson Family Papers: Byfield Mills, Box 1, folder 1, item 1, Phillips Library, Peabody Essex Museum, Salem, Massachusetts.

41. Pearson Family Papers: Miscellaneous, Box 1, folder 1, item 1, Phillips Library, Peabody Essex Museum, Salem, Massachusetts.

42. Pearson Family Papers: Miscellaneous, Box 1, folder 2, items 4–10, Phillips Library, Peabody Essex Museum, Salem, Massachusetts.

43. The Pearson ledgers were described in detail in George Brainard Blodgett, *Early Settlers of Rowley, Massachusetts*, (Rowley: Amos Everett Jewett, 1933), p. 272–3. Only one of these ledgers appears to have survived intact to the present. Pearson Family Account Book, MSS:446 (1684–1799), P361, V.1, Baker Library, Harvard, Cambridge, Massachusetts.

NOTES TO CHAPTER FIVE

1. William Harris, RIHS Collections, Vol. X, pg. 147.

2. Interview with Rabbit Goody, 27 July, 2001, Cooperstown, New York. "When I think of vernacular, I think below 50 ends and 50 picks; when I think trained weaver, I think 50s to 60s. Imported generally was 60s and above.

3. Virginia Anderson, *New England's Generation: The Great Migration and the Formation of Society and Culture in the Seventeenth Century*, p. 131.

4. James Duncan Phillips, *Salem in the Eighteenth Century*, (Boston: Houghton Mifflin, 1937), p. 78.

5. Phillip English Accounts, Box 17, MSS 11, English–Touzel–Hathorne Papers, Peabody Essex Museum, Salem, MA.

6. Phillip English Accounts, Box 17, folder 3. (loose leaves)

7. William Bowditch inventory, MSS 156, Box 1, File 1, Bowditch Family Collection, Peabody Essex Museum, Salem, MA.

8. John Touzell Account Book, English–Touzel–Hathorne Papers, Peabody Essex Museum, Salem, MA.

9. *New England's First Fruits*, Reprinted in Massachusetts Historical Society Collections, (Cambridge: Massachusetts Historical Society, 1792–1915).

10. Christopher Leffingwell Account Book, 1698–1714, Connecticut Historical Society Archive, West Hartford, CT.

11. Information on sail types provided by John Newman, Salem Maritime Museum, Salem, MA.
12. Christopher Leffingwell Account Book, 1698–1714, p. 27–28.
13. See Dorothy Burnham, *Cut My Cote*, (Toronto: Royal Ontario Museum, 1977).
14. Will of George Fenwick, *A Digest of Early Connecticut Probate Records*, Vol. I., Appendix, p. 52.
15. Will of George Fenwick, *A Digest of Early Connecticut Probate Records*, Vol. I., Appendix, p. 51–55.
16. Joseph Olmstead Account Book, 1685–1747, Connecticut Historical Society Archive, West Hartford, CT.
17. Will and Probate Record of Hillard Veren, Jr, *ECPR*, Vol. III, p. 362–366.
18. Inventory of Robert Wilkes, *ECPR*, Vol. III, p. 179–180.
19. Inventory of Phebe Eaton, *ECPR*, Vol. II, P. 342–343.

Bibliography

A. PRIMARY SOURCES

I. Unpublished Manuscripts

Barnard, Reverend Thomas. Diary. Barnard Family Collection, James Duncan Phillips Library, Peabody Essex Museum, Salem, Massachusetts.

Berkeley, Peter. Account Book, 1680–1683. Connecticut Historical Society Archive. East Hartford, Connecticut.

Bowditch, William. Bowditch Family Collection. Peabody Essex Museum, Salem, Massachusetts.

Buffum, Joshua. Account Book, 1674–1704. Buffum Family Manuscripts.James Duncan Phillips Library, Peabody Essex Museum, Salem, Massachusetts.

Byfield Mills. Pearson Family Papers. James Duncan Phillips Library, Peabody Essex Museum, Salem, Massachusetts.

Curwin, George. Account Books. Curwin Family Papers. James Duncan Phillips Library, Peabody Essex Museum, Salem, Massachusetts.

Ellis, Francis. Letterbook. Ellis Papers. James Duncan Phillips Library, Peabody Essex Museum, Salem, Massachusetts.

English, Phillip. Account Book. English–Touzel–Hathorne Papers. James Duncan Phillips Library, Peabody Essex Museum, Salem, Massachusetts.

Gould, John. Account Book, Gould Family Collection. James Duncan Phillips Library, Peabody Essex Museum, Salem, Massachusetts.

Holman, Winifred. Trial Documents. Middlesex County Superior Court Folio Collection. Massachusetts Archives, Columbia Point, Boston, Massachusetts.

Ingersol, Samuel. Account Book. James Duncan Phillips Library, Peabody Essex Museum, Salem, Massachusetts.

Ipswich Town Records, 1634–1662. Manuscript copy. James Duncan Phillips Library, Peabody Essex Museum, Salem, Massachusetts.

Ipswich Town Records, 1634–1720. Ipswich Town Clerk's Office. Ipswich, Massachusetts.

Judd, Sylvestor. Judd Manscripts. Forbes Library, Northampton, Massachusetts.

Leffingwell, Christopher. Account Book, 1698–1714. Connecticut Historical Society Archive. East Hartford, Connecticut.

Nantucket Account Book. Special Collections. University of Massachusetts Library. Amherst, Massachusetts.

Pearson, Jeremiah. Pearson Family Account Books, 1684–1689. Baker Library Archives. Harvard Business School. Cambridge, Massachusetts.

Pearson Miscellaneous Papers. Pearson Family Papers. James Duncan Phillips Library, Peabody-Essex Museum, Salem, Massachusetts.

Olmstead, Joseph. Account Book, 1685–1747. Connecticut Historical Society Archive. East Hartford, Connecticut.

Records and Files of the Quarterly Courts of Essex County, Massachusetts. WPA Transcripts. James Duncan Phillips Library, Peabody Essex Museum, Salem, Massachusetts.

Records and Files of the Quarterly Courts of Suffolk County. Microfilm copy. University of Massachusetts Library, Amherst, Massachusetts.

Standish, Loara. Sampler, c. 1640–50. Plymouth Hall Museum. Plymouth, Massachusetts.

Snow, Pamela Jean. Catle, Kine and rotherbeasts: Cattle and the plantation of Massachusetts, 1624–1684. M.A. Thesis. University of Maine, 1998.

Suffolk County Probate Records, Vol. I-IX. Unpublished Microfilm. University of Massachusetts Library, Amherst, Massachusetts.

Taylor, Samuel. Barton Family Manuscripts. James Duncan Phillips Library, Peabody Essex Museum, Salem, Massachusetts.

Touzel, John. Account Book. English–Touzel–Hathorne Papers. James Duncan Phillips Library, Peabody Essex Museum, Salem, Massachusetts.

II. Published Sources

Abbott, Lemuel Abijah. *Descendants of George Abbott of Rowley, Massachusetts.* Rowley: n.p., 1906.

Bishop, J. Leander. *A History of American Manufactures.* Philadelphia: E. Young and Son, 1868.

Blodgett, George Brainard. *Early Settlers of Rowley, Massachusetts.* Rowley: Amos Everette Jewett, 1933.

Boyer, Paul and Nissenbaum, Stephen, eds. *The Salem Witchcraft Papers: Verbatim Transcripts of the Legal Documents of the Salem Witchcraft Outbreak of 1692.* New York: 1977.

———, eds. *Salem Witchcraft: A Documentary Record of Local Conflict in Colonial New England.* Boston: Northeastern University Press, 1993.

Eliot, Jared. *Essays Upon Field Husbandry in New England, As It Is Or May Be Ordered.* Boston: Edes and Gill, 1762.

Essex County Probate Records, 1635–1681. Salem: The Essex Institute, 1917.

Gleanings from the Most Celebrated Books on Husbandry, Gardening and Rural Affairs. Philadelphia: James Humphreys, 1803.

Hambrick-Stowe, Charles E. *Early New England Meditative Poetry.* New York: Paulist Press, 1988.

Hosmer, James K. *Winthrop's Journal, 1630–1649.* New York: 1903.

Hurd, Hamilton. *History of Middlesex County, Massachusetts.* Philadelphia: J.W. Lewis & Co., 1890.

Johnson, Edward. *Wonder-Working Providence of Sions Savior in New England.* London, 1654.

Knight, Sarah. *The Journal of Madame Knight.* New York: Peter Smith, 1935.

Lincoln, Charles H., ed. *The Narratives of the Indian Wars, 1675–1699.* New York: Charles Scribner's Sons, 1913.

Manwaring, Charles. *A Digest of the Early Connecticut Probate Records.* Hartford: R.S. Peck & Co., 1904.

Marblehead Town Records, 1648–1683. Salem: Essex Institute, 1933.

Maverick, Samuel. *A Briefe Description of New England and the Townes Therein Together With the Present Government, 1660.* Reprinted in Boston: David Clapp & Son, 1885.

New England's First Fruits. Reprinted in *Massachusetts Historical Society Collections.* Cambridge: Massachusetts Historical Society, 1792–1915.

Records and Files of the Quarterly Courts of Essex County, Massachusetts. Salem: Essex Institute, 1912–75.

Rowley Town Records. Rowley, Massachusetts: n.p., 1894.

Salem Town Records, 1634–1691. Microfiche. Library of American Civilization. LAC20507.

Simmons, C. H., Ed. *Plymouth Colony Records, 1633–1669.* Camden, Maine: Picton Press, 1996.

Shurtleff, Nathaniel, ed. *Records of the Governor and Company of the Massachusetts Bay in New England.* Boston: M. White, 1853–4.

Torrey, Clarence Almon. *New England Marriages Prior to 1700.* Baltimore: Genealogical Publishing Company, Inc., 1985.

Tusser, Thomas. *Five Hundred Points of Good Husbandry.* 1580 edition. London: Lackington, Allen & Co., 1812.

Upham, William P. "Records of Salem, 1634–1659." *Essex Institute Historical Collections.* Salem: Essex Institute, 1868.

Wily, John. *A Treatise on the Propagation of Sheep, the Manufacture of Wool, and the Cultivation and Manufacture of Flax.* Williamsburg, Virginia: 1765.

B. SECONDARY SOURCES

I. Articles

Park, Helen. "Thomas Dennis, Ipswich Joiner: A Re-examination." *Antiques.* LXXVII (July, 1960):40–44.

Park, Helen. "The Seventeenth-Century Furniture of Essex County and Its Makers." *Antiques.* LXXVII (October, 1960):350–355.

Rediker, Marcus. "Good Hands, Stout Heart, and Fast Feet: The History and Culture of Working People in early America." *Labour/Le Travailleur.* Autumn, 1982: 123–144.

Trautman, Patricia. "Dress in Seventeenth-Century Cambridge, Massachusetts: An Inventory-Based Reconstruction." *Dublin Seminar For New England Folklife Annual Proceedings.* Peter Benes, ed. Boston: Boston University, 1989:51–73.

II. Monographs

Anderson, Virginia. *Creatures of Empire*. New York: Oxford University Press, 2004.

————. *New England's Generation: The Great Migration and the Formation of Society and Culture in the Seventeenth Century*. Cambridge: Cambridge University Press, 1991.

Bagnall, William. *The Textile Industries of the United States Including Sketches of Cotton, Woolen, Silk, and Linen Manufactures in the Colonial Period*. Boston: W.B. Clarke, 1893.

Bailyn, Bernard. *The New England Merchants in the Seventeenth Century*. New York: Harper and Row, 1964.

Boydston, Jeanne. *Home and Work: Housework, Wages, and the Ideology of Labor in the Early Republic*. New York: Oxford University Press, 1990.

Bridenbaugh, Carl. *Fat Mutton and Liberty of Conscience: Society in Rhode Island, 1636–1690*. Rhode Island: Brown University Press, 1974.

Burnham, Dorothy. *Cut my Cote*. Toronto: Royal Ontario Museum, 1977.

Clark, Alice. *Working Life of Women in the Seventeenth Century*. London: George Routledge and Sons, 1919.

Connor, Louis G. *A Brief History of Sheep Industry in the United States*. Washington, D.C.: GPO, 1921.

Demos, John. *A Little Commonwealth: Family Life in Plymouth Colony*. Oxford: Oxford University Press, 1970.

Donohue, Brian. *Reclaiming the Commons: Community Farms and Forests in a New England Town*. New Haven & London: Yale University Press, 1999.

Fales, Dean A. *Essex County Furniture: Documented Treasures from Local Collections, 1660–1860*. Salem: Essex Institute, 1965.

Holmes, Abiel. *The Annals of America from the Discovery by Columbus in 1492 to the year 1826*. Cambridge: Hilliard and Brown, 1829.

Innes, Stephen, ed. *Work and Labor in Early America*. Chapel Hill: University of North Carolina Press, 1988.

Jenson, Joan. *Loosening the Bonds: Mid-Atlantic Farm Women, 1750–1850*. New Haven: Yale University Press, 1986.

Karlsen, Carol. *Devil in the Shape of a Woman: Witchcraft in Colonial New England*. New York: W.W. Norton & Co., 1987.

Katz, Stanley and Murrin, John, eds. *Colonial America: Essays in Politics and Social Development*. New York: Alfred A. Knopf, 1983.

McCusker, John J. and Menard, Russell R. *The Economy of British America, 1607–1789*. Chapel Hill: University of North Carolina Press, 1991.

Montgomery, Florence M. *Textiles in America, 1650–1870*. New York: W.W. Norton, 1984.

Phillips, James Duncan. *Salem in the Eighteenth Century*. Boston: Houghton Mifflin, 1937.

Tarule, Robert. *The Artisan of Ipswich*. Baltimore: The Johns Hopkins Press, 2004.

Thompson, Roger. *Mobility and Migration: East Anglian Founders of New England, 1629–1640*. Amherst: University of Massachusetts Press, 1994.

Ulrich, Laurel Thatcher. *Age of Homespun: Objects and Stories in the Creation of An American Myth*. New York: Alfred A. Knopf, 2001.

————. *Good Wives: Image and Reality in the Lives of Women in Northern New England, 1650–1750*. New York: Alfred A. Knopf, 1982

————. *A Midwife's Tale: The Life of Martha Ballard Based on Her Diary, 1785–1812*. New York: Alfred A. Knopf, 1990.

Vickers, Daniel. *Farmers and Fishermen: Two Centuries of Work in Essex County, Massachusetts, 1630–1850*. Chapel Hill: University of North Carolina Press, 1994.

Wadsworth, A. P. & Julia D. L. Mann. *The Cotton Trade and Industrial Lancashire, 1600–1780*. Manchester: Manchester University Press, 1931.

Waters, Thomas Franklyn. *Ipswich in the Massachusetts Bay Colony*. Ipswich: Ipswich Historical Society, 1905.

Whitman, Edmund. *Flax Culture: An Outline of the History and Present Condition of the Flax Industry in the United States*. Boston: Rand Avery Company, 1888.

Index